The SECRET Court Martial of Admiral Kimmel

Pearl Harbor Revisited

A Courtroom Drama

by

James Edwin Alexander
William R. Burkett

Macedon

ISBN 0-939965-28-3

The paper in this book meets the guidelines for permanence and durability of the Committee on Production Guidelines for Book Longevity of the Council on Library Resources, Inc.

1 2 3 4 5 6 7 8 9 10

Preface

This Court Martial never took place. But it should have.

Admiral Husband E. Kimmel was Commander-in-Chief of the U.S. Fleet at Pearl Harbor in 1941. He bore the brunt of the blame for the December 7 Japanese surprise attack. Shortly after the Pearl Harbor, he was relieved of his command and reverted back to his permanent rank of two-star Rear Admiral. When it became clear that he would not be assigned to another command, Admiral Kimmel took retirement. He spent the rest of World War II in the service of Harris Engineering Company.

No formal charges were ever filed against Admiral Kimmel. Nevertheless, he was judged guilty in the court of public opinion.

A total of nine investigations (Knox, Roberts, Hart, NCI, APHB, Clarke, Clausen, Hewitt, and JCC) were held between 1941 and 1946 to investigate the causes of the Pearl Harbor disaster. Except in the case of the Naval Court of Inquiry in 1944, in all other investigations Admiral Kimmel was not allowed to call witnesses in his defense or to cross-examine witnesses who testified in other proceedings.

Admiral Kimmel requested he be given a court martial. He even waived the statute of limitations in order that one might be held. Admiral King rejected that request also, commenting that there was not sufficient evidence to convict.

In 1945-46, a Joint Congressional Hearing, generally known as the "Pearl Harbor Hearing," provided a great service for future historians. It bound up in its proceedings the transcripts of all previous hearings. The report runs to 39 volumes of tightly packed text and is available in government repositories.

In what may be termed an act of foolhardiness, we have decided to give Admiral Kimmel the court martial he had always requested but was never granted.

In staging this trial, we have relied on the transcripts of the Hart Inquiry conducted at Pearl Harbor in the spring of 1944, presided over by Admiral Thomas C. Hart; of the Naval Court of Inquiry conducted in the summer of 1944, presided over by Admiral Orin G. Murfin; and of the Joint Congressional Investigation conducted in Washington in 1945-46, presided over by Senator (and later Vice-President) Alben Barkley.

More than forty witnesses testified at length in these hearings. To accommodate the limited time available to us in this format, we have limited the cast to 14 witnesses. The reader may find several places where the grammar is poor or sentence structure is awkward. For the most part, these inconsistencies are due to the hearings' transcripts themselves.

People on the witness stand do not always speak with perfect grammar or in complete sentences. We have on occasion taken literary license to shorten, clarify and animate the testimony, always being strictly faithful to the essence of what was transcribed, and never altering the theme, nature or intent of those who testified. The testimony so attributed is always in character and within the knowledge of the attributee, and it is how we believe he would have answered had he been asked the question.

Except for the courtroom setting itself, all the witnesses are real, and their testimony is real.

James Edwin Alexander
William R. Burkett
September 2002

This drama is dedicated to
Admiral Husband E. Kimmel
and his family

CAST OF CHARACTERS

IN ORDER OF APPEARANCE

ADMIRAL HUSBAND E. KIMMEL (Defendant)

ADMIRAL CHARLES DANFORTH (Defense Attorney)

VICE ADMIRAL JOHN PROCTOR (Judge Advocate)

ADMIRAL FRANK COURTNEY (President of the Court)

ADMIRAL HAROLD R. STARK (Witness)

REAR ADMIRAL R.B. INGLIS (Witness)

VICE ADMIRAL P.N.L. BELLINGER (Witness)

VICE ADMIRAL RICHMOND K. TURNER (Witness)

REAR ADMIRAL T.S. WILKINSON (Witness)

REAR ADMIRAL LEIGH NOYES (Witness)

CAPTAIN A.D. KRAMER (Witness)

CAPTAIN L.F. SAFFORD (Witness)

CAPTAIN ARTHUR M. McCOLLUM (Witness)

CAPTAIN JOSEPH J. ROCHEFORT (Witness)

VICE ADMIRAL WILLIAM S. PYE (Witness)

ADMIRAL CLAUDE C. BLOCH (Witness)

LT. COL. KERMIT A. TYLER (Witness)

VICE ADMIRAL WILLIAM F. HALSEY (Witness)

(4) ADMIRALS (Members of the Court)

STENOGRAPHER

ORDERLY

ACT ONE: The Prosecution

ACT TWO: The Defense

ACT THREE: The Verdict

The time of this play is July 1944. The scene is a Court Martial room at the 14th District Naval Headquarters in Pearl Harbor, T.H.

THE SCENE: The curtain is up when the audience enters the theater. The stage is dimly lit. A raised JUDGE's bench with seating for five judges is at Stage Left, with the WITNESS Chair adjacent to it and a large American flag draped behind. Upstage right is the JUDGE ADVOCATE'S desk, with one chair behind it. Downstage right is the DEFENDANT'S table with two chairs. A lectern (podium) stands at Stage Center. A small desk for the STENOGRAPHER is Upstage from the Judge's Bench. Placed out of the way, near the entrance to the stage, is a chair for the ORDERLY.

ACT I: The Prosecution

The start of the play is marked by the participants entering and taking their places. Stage remains dim.

Enter CHARLES DANFORTH and ADMIRAL KIMMEL. They cross to their desk. DANFORTH puts briefcase down. KIMMEL leans over to talk with DANFORTH.

JOHN PROCTOR enters, crosses to his desk, puts briefcase down.

Enter four ADMIRALS, the STENOGRAPHER, and the ORDERLY, who take their places.
All officers are in dress whites. Witnesses are in dress blues.

House lights dim, and Stage brightens.

ORDERLY: All rise!

All stand to attention as Admiral FRANK COURTNEY enters and goes to his place in silence.

COURTNEY: The Court will come to order. Be seated, please.

All sit.

COURTNEY: I need not remind you that this nation is still at war. Because of the overriding requirement of secrecy concerning our ability to conduct war against Japan, this trial will be closed to the public. No reporters, visitors, or other unauthorized personnel will be present during the trial, nor will you discuss matters pertaining to this trial with anyone whatsoever outside this courtroom.

All nod.

COURTNEY: *(Holds out paper to PROCTOR.)* Court finds the charge and specification in due form and technically correct. Is the accused ready for trial?

Kimmel rises.

KIMMEL: Yes, sir.

COURTNEY nods to PROCTOR, who reads from the paper.

PROCTOR: "Charge: Dereliction of duty. Specification (1) In that Admiral Husband E. Kimmel failed to use patrol aircraft that were available to him on or about December 7, 1941, to conduct long range reconnaissance in the more dangerous sectors around Pearl Harbor; (2) Admiral Husband E. Kimmel failed to rotate the 'in port' periods of his ships in a less routine manner so as to have made it impossible for the Japanese to predict when there would be vessels in port; (3) Admiral Husband E. Kimmel failed to appreciate the gravity of the situation even a few hours before the Japanese attack on Pearl Harbor, whereby his naval planes would have been in the air during the early morning period and his ships' batteries would have been fully manned."

COURTNEY: Husband E. Kimmel, Rear Admiral, retired, U.S. Navy, you have heard the charge and specifications preferred against you, how say you, guilty or not guilty?

KIMMEL: Not guilty.

COURTNEY: Very well, your plea is accepted. Judge Advocate, you may present your case.

PROCTOR: If it please the Court, all exhibits have been exchanged by the parties, and the parties have stipulated that, subject to the approval of the Court, all exhibits may be admitted at this time.

COURTNEY: So ordered.

PROCTOR: The prosecution calls Admiral Harold Stark

ENTER Admiral Stark, an average man of average height, white hair, wire-rim glasses, who could be mistaken for a middle-aged shopkeeper, raises his hand to be sworn.

COURTNEY: You do solemnly swear that the evidence you shall give in this court shall be the truth, the whole truth, and nothing but the truth. So help you God.

STARK: I do.

Takes the witness chair.

PROCTOR: Will you state your name, rank, and present station?

STARK: Harold R. Stark, Admiral, U.S. Navy, Commanding U.S. Naval Forces, European waters.

PROCTOR: What were your duties August 1939 to March 1942?

STARK: Chief of Naval Operations.

PROCTOR: What is the name of the officer who was in command of the U.S. Pacific Fleet on 7 December 1941?

STARK: Admiral Husband E. Kimmel.

PROCTOR: During the two or three months preceding 7 December 1941, who were your principal advisors, assistants, or aides in the Navy Department?

STARK: My assistants and advisors at that time were Admiral Royal E. Ingersoll; the Assistant Chief of Naval Operations; Admiral Kelly Turner, Head of War Plans; Admiral T.S. Wilkinson, Head of Office of Naval Intelligence; and Admiral Leah Noyes, Communications Division. Those were the principal ones as I can recall at the moment.

PROCTOR: Will you state in general the principal duties of Admiral Ingersoll?

STARK: Admiral Ingersoll was my close assistant. He took off my shoulders many matters of detail which he settled himself.

PROCTOR: Will you tell the court in general what the principal duties of Admiral Turner were?

STARK: Admiral Turner, as head of the War Plans Division, was charged with the drawing up of plans for the use of the Fleet in war. He worked very closely with Army War Plans. He kept in very close touch with the disposition made in connection with War Plans. I think that may cover the broad outline of it.

PROCTOR: Would you call Admiral Turner your principal military advisor?

STARK: Most definitely. I think there is no exaggeration to state that we were in what might be called constant conference on important military problems. I saw him not only daily, but frequently a number of times daily.

PROCTOR: What were the principal duties of Admiral Wilkinson?

STARK: His principal duty was the collection and dissemination of information, and of course keeping me informed of what was regarded as important and pertinent.

PROCTOR: I show you, sir, a document which has been marked for identification as EXHIBIT 1. Do you recognize this document?

STARK: I do, as Navy Basic War Plan WPL-46.

PROCTOR: Was the document in effect on December 7, 1941?

STARK: The document had been promulgated, but had not yet been executed until a formal declaration of war.

PROCTOR: What was the major task of the Pacific Fleet assigned in this War Plan?

STARK: (Reading) *"Protect the territory of the associated powers in the Pacific area and prevent the extension of enemy military power in the western hemisphere by destroying hostile expeditions and by supporting land and sea forces in denying the enemy the use of land positions in that hemisphere."*

PROCTOR: Did you write any letters, notes, or memoranda to Admiral Kimmel, setting forth the view of the Navy Department on the probability of war between the United States and Japan?

STARK: I wrote on the 23rd of September. There is a paragraph in that letter that refers to Admiral Nomura, the Japanese Ambassador.

PROCTOR: That is marked EXHIBIT 2. Will you read extracts which are responsive to the question?

STARK: (Reading) *"Admiral Nomura came in to see me this morning. We talked about an hour. He usually comes in when he begins to feel near the end of his rope. There is not much to spare at the end now. If negotiations fall through, and it looks like they might, the situation could only grow more tense"*

PROCTOR: Sir, I hand you a photostatic copy, duly authenticated under official seal and marked EXHIBIT 3, of a dispatch from the Chief of Naval Operations to the Commander-in-Chief, of the Pacific Fleet, dated 16 October 1941. Please state if you can identify it.

STARK. I can.

PROCTOR: What special circumstances prompted your sending this dispatch to you Admiral Kimmel?

STARK: The resignation of the Japanese cabinet, which the dispatch states, which did in our opinion create a grave situation.

PROCTOR: Will you read the next-to-last sentence of this dispatch?

STARK: (Reading:) *"In view of the possibilities, you will take precautions including such preparatory deployments as will not disclose strategic intentions or constitute provocative actions against Japan."*

PROCTOR: I hand you a photostatic copy from the Chief of Naval Operations to the Commander-in-Chief, Pacific and other addressees, dated 24 November 1941, marked EXHIBIT 4. Please state if you recognize it.

STARK: Yes, I recognize it.

PROCTOR: What special circumstances prompted your sending it?

STARK: Primarily, it looked less and less as though favorable outcome of the negotiations with Japan would be forthcoming. In my opinion the situation was deteriorating. In addition, the Japs were moving into Formosa. You will note that the dispatch says that *"a surprise, aggressive movement in any direction, including an attack on the Philippines or Guam is a possibility."*

PROCTOR: Do you recall whether you felt at the time an attack on Pearl Harbor was a possibility?

STARK: Yes, I thought it was a possibility. That was the reason I wrote the words, "in any direction."

PROCTOR: Admiral, I hand you what has been marked EXHIBIT 5, a photostatic copy of a dispatch from the Chief of Naval Operations to the Commander-in-Chief, Pacific Fleet, and other addressees, dated November 27, 1941. Do you identify this document as such?

STARK: I recognize it as the so-called "war warning" message.

PROCTOR: What additional information had you received between November 24 and November 27, 1941, that prompted your sending this dispatch?

STARK: Negotiations with Japan had come to an impasse; they were stopped. I pondered a great deal over the expression, *"this is a war warning,"* with my principal advisors. We thought there was grave danger of Japan striking somewhere and we wanted the outlying stations to know, and we used language strong enough to indicate to them that Japan was going to strike.

PROCTOR: Can you state what action you expected the Commander-in-Chief of the Pacific Fleet to take in receipt of your dispatch of 27 November 1941?

STARK: Very briefly, I expected full readiness measures ashore and afloat, distance reconnaissance and anti-submarine measures. I assumed that all measures previously agreed upon for emergency would be implemented.

PROCTOR: In your dispatch of October 16, 1941, you directed the Commander-in-Chief of the Pacific Fleet to take due precautions, including preparatory deployments that will not constitute provocative action. In your dispatch of 27 November 1941, you directed addressees to execute an appropriate defense deployment preparatory to carrying out the tasks assigned in WPL-46. Now, what additional dispositions of the forces assigned to the Commander-in-Chief of the Pacific Fleet were intended in this last directive?

STARK: Keeping in mind the words "war warning," I would assume full security measures, not only for ships in port but for ships at sea; measures regarding the safety of Pearl Harbor; anti-submarine measures; distance reconnaissance; and that they should be fully alive to the possibility of war and that watches would be placed on such basis.

PROCTOR: On either the 6th or 7th of December,

1941, did you receive any further information on diplomatic developments with the Japanese Government?

STARK: On Sunday forenoon, the 7th, there was information to the effect that the Japanese Ambassador was to call on the Secretary of State at exactly 1300 hours. I was talking this over with Captain Schuirmann when General Marshall called me asking me if I had it. I told him "yes," and he asked me what I thought about sending it on to the Hawaiian Islands. To the best of my memory, my first answer to him was that we had sent them so much already and of such a character that I questioned sending this information. I hung up the phone, and I think within a minute I called him back and said I would go along with his hunch that it might be a good thing to send that information to the Pacific. I told him to go ahead and be sure and embody in his dispatch to inform our people, that is, the Navy at Pearl.

PROCTOR: Let me hand you EXHIBIT 6, which is a letter from the Secretary of the Navy to the Secretary of War, dated January 24, 1941. Will you read therefrom the dangers envisaged in the order of their importance?

STARK: (Reading) *"(1) air bombing attack; (2) air torpedo attack; (3) sabotage; (4) submarine attack; (5) mining; (6) bombardment by gunfire."*

PROCTOR: In this letter of January 24, 1941, an air

torpedo plane attack was placed No. 2 on the list of dangers envisaged. Assuming that an air torpedo attack was imminent, what do you consider the relative merits of the safety of the U.S. Fleet in Pearl Harbor as contrasted with a similar attack on the Fleet at sea?

STARK: I would consider the danger of the Fleet in Pearl Harbor would be greater than it would be against the Fleet at sea.

PROCTOR: I show you a letter marked EXHIBIT 7. Can you identify it?

STARK: Yes. It is a letter from the Commandant of the 14th Naval District to the Chief of Naval Operations, dated 1 May 1941. Subject, Air Defense of Pearl Harbor.

PROCTOR: Will you identify Enclosure C of this letter?

STARK: It is a joint estimate covering joint Army and Navy air action in the event of sudden hostile action against Oahu, and it is signed by Rear Admiral P.N.L. Bellinger and General F.L. Martin.

PROCTOR: Admiral, will you read from that, Appendix C, Article 3, sub-paragraphs (a) and (b)?

STARK: (Reading): *"Article 3: Possible enemy action. (a) A declaration of war might be preceded by: (1) A surprise submarine attack on ships in the oper-*

ating area, (2) A surprise attack on Oahu, including ships and installations in Pearl Harbor, (3) A combination of these two. (b) It appears that the most likely and dangerous form of attack on Oahu would be an air attack. It is believed that at present such an attack would probably be launched from one or more carriers, which would probably approach inside 300 miles."

PROCTOR: Thank you, Admiral. I have no further questions.

PROCTOR returns to his desk. DANFORTH approaches podium, yellow pad in his hand.

DANFORTH: Good morning, Admiral. My name is Charles Danforth. I represent Admiral Kimmel. I have just a couple of questions I'd like to ask to clarify something you said.

STARK: (Nods)

DANFORTH: Would you agree with me, Admiral, that it is not the purpose of this trial to assign blame for the surprise attack on Pearl Harbor, but to determine if Admiral Kimmel is guilty of the charge brought against him, namely, dereliction of duty and disobedience of orders?

STARK: Yes, I would agree with you. *(Appears annoyed)*

DANFORTH: Thank you. Now, on the morning of

December 7, when you learned from General Marshall and the Navy Department that the Japanese government had instructed its ambassador to meet with the Secretary of State at 1300 hours, did you attach any significance to the hour of 1 p.m. Washington time?

STARK: We didn't know. We thought there might be something, and in view of this "might," that we ought not to take any chances and we decided to send a message to the outlying stations.

DANFORTH: Admiral, 1300 hours Washington time is what time in Honolulu?

STARK: 0730.

DANFORTH: Admiral, what time did the first Japanese attack begin?

STARK: Approximately 0753, Honolulu time.

DANFORTH: Did you or any member of your staff follow up to make sure the message was received in Hawaii?

STARK: We did not.

DANFORTH: Turning now to your dispatch of October 16, when you used the word "possibility," you wrote Admiral Kimmel that you personally did not believe that the Japs were going to sail into us?

STARK: I did.

DANFORTH: When you used the word "possibility" in your dispatch of November 24, did you use it with the same connotation?

STARK: I still was not convinced that it was more than a possibility.

DANFORTH: And you have testified in your dispatch of November 24th, the words "in any direction" expressed your thought that an attack on Pearl Harbor was a possibility?

STARK: That is right.

DANFORTH: As a matter of fact, didn't you consider an attack on Pearl Harbor as no more than a possibility, even on November 27?

STARK: I considered it as a possibility.

DANFORTH: But a rather remote possibility?

STARK: Well, I went between "remote possibility" and "probability." It is a little hard to differentiate. I considered it a possibility.

DANFORTH: You did not consider it a probability?

STARK: No, I did not consider it a probability. If I had thought it a probability, I would have mentioned it. I thought it a possibility.

DANFORTH: My question was, If you had conceived Pearl Harbor to be a probable point of attack, you would have included it specifically in your message of November 27?

STARK: If I had information that indicated Pearl Harbor was a point of attack, I certainly would have included it.

DANFORTH: On direct, you cited the Martin-Bellinger report, EXHIBIT 7. Let me read to you, Admiral Stark, paragraph 4 of that report. (Reading:) *"Run daily patrols as far as possible to seaward through 360 degrees to reduce the probabilities of surface or air surprise. This would be desirable but can only be effectively maintained with present personnel and material for a very short period and as a practical measure cannot, therefore, be undertaken unless other intelligence indicates that a surface raid is probable within rather narrow time limits."* Did you send Admiral Kimmel any intelligence that a surface raid on Pearl Harbor was probable within rather narrow time limits?

STARK: We had no intelligence to that effect.

DANFORTH: I ask if you can identify EXHIBIT 8 as a photostatic copy of a letter written by Admiral Kimmel to you dated 18 February 1941?

STARK: I recognize this letter.

DANFORTH: Did you understand from the postscript that Admiral Kimmel requested to be promptly advised as to information of a secret nature?

STARK: Which would be of use to him, yes.

DANFORTH: Did you understand the request to include all information relative to diplomatic and international developments affecting the Pacific Area?

STARK: I would say, not all matters. We aimed to keep the Commander-in-Chief in the Pacific acquainted with these subjects, so far as we thought he would have a vital interest, but to have sent him a mass of everything that came in without evaluation, it might have been more of a hindrance than help to him.

DANFORTH: The only reason you would not send him information in that category was that you felt it too trivial to be worthy of his attention?

STARK: Well, I wouldn't send him that which I thought to be trivial of his attention.

DANFORTH: I show you EXHIBIT 9, a letter from Admiral Kimmel, to the Chief of Naval Operations, dated 26 May 1941, and ask that you identify it.

STARK: Yes, I recall that correspondence.

DANFORTH: Will you read, Admiral Stark, the last sentence of paragraph seven?

STARK: (Reading:) *"It is suggested that it be made a cardinal principle that the Commander-in-Chief, Pacific Fleet, be immediately informed of all important developments as they occur and by the quickest means available."*

DANFORTH: In fact, you fully agreed with his suggestion, didn't you?

STARK: Yes. And to the best of my conscience I did.

DANFORTH: You are now conscious of no important development of which Admiral Kimmel was not advised by the quickest means then available?

STARK: I have searched my brain, my conscience, my heart, and everything I have got, since Pearl Harbor started, to see wherein I might have been derelict or wherein I might have omitted something. There is only one thought—in my mind there is only one thought that I regretted. What the effect would have been, I don't know—that was the dispatch which was sent by the Army on the morning of December 7, that I had not paralleled it with my own system, or that I had not telephoned it. I may be reminded, before this trial is over, of other things where I may realize that there was something more that I could have done, but that is the one conscious realization I remember and regret.

DANFORTH: One final question, Admiral. Did you consider war imminent?

STARK: Yes, we were looking for Japan to strike any day. We didn't know where.

DANFORTH: You never advised Admiral Kimmel in so many words that war was imminent?

STARK: I thought I had; I intended to.

DANFORTH: The words "imminence of war" were not included in any of Admiral Kimmel's dispatches, were they?

STARK: Well, I think the equivalent was. The dispatch stated that this was a war warning and that an aggressive move by Japan was expected within the next few days, and from the best indications we had, it would be the Philippines, Thailand, the Kra Peninsula, or possibly Borneo.

DANFORTH: But Hawaii was not mentioned?

STARK: Hawaii was not mentioned.

DANFORTH: Finally, Admiral Stark, when Admiral Kimmel was appointed Commander-in-Chief of the Pacific Fleet in February 1941, did you have and express an opinion about his selection?

STARK: I strongly recommended his appointment.

He was my choice, my recommendation. I do not mean by that, that others did not recommend him. Many did.

DANFORTH: I hand you, sir, what has been marked as EXHIBIT 10. Can you identify it?

STARK: I identify it as a report of the fitness of Rear Admiral Husband E. Kimmel, Commander-in-Chief, United States Fleet, from the period 1 October 1941 to December 17, 1941.

DANFORTH: Please read, sir, question 14 and your answer.

STARK: (Reading:) *"Number 14. Is this officer professionally qualified to perform ALL the duties of his grade? Answer: I have always considered Admiral Kimmel an outstanding officer in ability, integrity and character. I still do."*

DANFORTH: Have you changed your mind?

STARK: Not in the least.

DANFORTH: Thank you. No further questions.

DANFORTH returns to his desk. PROCTOR indicates he does not desire to question witness further.

COURTNEY: Admiral, you are excused but only for the time being. You may be recalled for such further questioning as the court may direct. You will remain under oath and are instructed not to discuss your testimony with any other person.

STARK: May it please the Court: I am under orders to return to my command post without delay, and must do so as soon as I can verify my testimony. My absence from the Court's proceedings is beyond my control.

COURTNEY: Very well, there being no objection, you are dismissed.

EXIT Admiral Stark

PROCTOR: Call Admiral Inglis.

ENTER: Admiral Inglis, a tall, scholarly, distinguished man, raises his right hand.

COURTNEY: You do solemnly swear that the testimony you are about to give will be the truth, the whole truth, and nothing but the truth. So help you God.

INGLIS: I do.

Takes witness chair.

PROCTOR: State your name.

INGLIS: T. B. Inglis, Rear Admiral, United States Navy.

PROCTOR: Admiral Inglis, what is your status in the Navy now?

INGLIS: I am attached to the Office of Naval Operations as Chief of Naval Intelligence.

PROCTOR: Have you prepared exhibits to clarify your testimony today?

INGLIS: I have, sir, with the assistance of officers under my control.

PROCTOR: Please give us a narrative statement of the conditions at Pearl Harbor on December 7, 1941, and what occurred there.

INGLIS: I propose to start this presentation with a brief description of the disposition of the ships at Pearl Harbor. I have prepared a chart for this purpose.

PROCTOR positions chart on easel so it is visible both to panel and Inglis.

PROCTOR: Referring to EXHIBIT 11, Admiral, what ships were in Pearl Harbor on December 7, 1941?

INGLIS: They are shown on the chart before the Court. Eight battleships were among the ships in the harbor that day, located as follows: May I approach the chart?

COURTNEY: You may.

INGLIS leaves the witness chair, takes position in front of large chart, picks up pointer.

INGLIS: (Pointing:) The *Nevada, Arizona, West Virginia, Tennessee, Oklahoma, Maryland,* and *California* were moored on the southeast side of Ford Island; the *Pennsylvania* in dry-dock No. 1 at the navy yard.

Two heavy cruisers, *New Orleans* and *San Francisco,* of the 10,000-ton type, were at the docks in the navy yard repair basin.

Four light cruisers of the 10,000-ton type were berthed as follows: *St. Louis, Honolulu, Helena* at navy yard docks, and *Phoenix* moored northeast of Ford Island.

Two light cruisers of the 7,000-ton type, *Raleigh* and *Detroit,* were on the northwest side of Ford Island.

Twenty-nine destroyers, all but three of which had been completed since 1933, were moored on the north and west of Ford Island.

There were five submarines, four of which were tied up at the submarine base, and the fifth at Ten-ten dock in the navy yard.

The dock is called Ten-ten dock because it is 1,010 feet long.

One gunboat was tied up at a navy yard dock. Nine minelayers, eight of which were converted flush-deck destroyers, were located at navy yard docks and in middle loch.

Eleven minesweepers, five of which were converted flush-deck destroyers, moored in middle loch and at navy yard docks.

Twenty-three fleet auxiliaries, such as repair ships, oilers, tenders, store ships, and tugs were located at various berths throughout the harbor.

There were no aircraft carriers in port.

All battleships of the Pacific Fleet except the *Colorado,* which was in the navy yard at Puget Sound, were present in Pearl Harbor.

In accordance with existing fleet orders, the vessels of the Pacific Fleet except those undergoing navy yard overhaul maintained condition of readiness 3 while in the harbor. This condition at that time varied according to the armaments of the various types of ships but, in general, required that about one-fourth of the antiaircraft batteries and necessary control stations be manned and that ready ammunition be at the guns. Vessels likewise were limited in the degree to which they could disable their propulsive machinery. In general, most vessels were on twelve hours' notice.

PROCTOR: And where were the aircraft carriers at this time?

INGLIS lays down pointer.

INGLIS: The *Lexington* was en route to Midway from Pearl to deliver fighter planes to the U.S. Marines; and the *Enterprise* was returning from delivering airplanes to Wake Island.

PROCTOR: Who was in charge of the *Lexington?*

INGLIS: The *Lexington* was in a task group with three heavy cruisers and five destroyers commanded by Admiral John Henry Newton. It was about 460 miles from Midway.

PROCTOR: What did Halsey have charge of—Admiral Halsey?

INGLIS: Admiral William Halsey had charge of the *Enterprise* group. It was accompanied by three heavy cruisers and nine destroyers.

PROCTOR: Where was the *Enterprise?*

INGLIS: Two hundred miles west of Pearl Harbor.

PROCTOR: You may return to your seat. Now Admiral, can you give the Court a report on the damages to the Fleet resulting from the Japanese attack?

INGLIS returns to witness chair.

INGLIS: Yes. (Reads from folder:)
Battleships: Sunk—*Arizona, California,* and *West Virginia.* Capsized—*Oklahoma.* Heavily dam-

aged—*Nevada.* Damaged—*Maryland, Pennsylvania, Tennessee.*

Light Cruisers: Heavily damaged—*Helena, Raleigh.* Damaged—*Honolulu.*

Destroyers: Heavily damaged—*Shaw, Cassin,* and *Downes.*

Auxiliaries: Badly damaged or sunk—*Vestal, Oglala, Curtis,* and *Utah.*

PROCTOR: Approximately two-thirds of the U.S. Pacific Fleet was in port on that fateful Sunday. Is that a fair statement?

INGLIS: Approximately, sir.

PROCTOR: Admiral, do you have an opinion as to whether the fleet should or should not have been concentrated in Pearl Harbor on Sunday morning, December 7, 1941?

INGLIS: I do not feel I am qualified to render an opinion.

PROCTOR: (Seems taken aback by the answer.) Thank you, Admiral. I have no further questions at this time.

PROCTOR returns to desk. DANFORTH moves to podium.

DANFORTH: Admiral Inglis, I believe you testified that the ships in Pearl Harbor were at condition 3 readiness?

INGLIS: Yes, sir.

DANFORTH: Which means that approximately one-fourth of the antiaircraft batteries are manned and that ready ammunition is at the guns?

INGLIS: That is correct.

DANFORTH: Now, Admiral Inglis, based on your knowledge and experience, would condition 3 be an appropriate level of readiness if the fleet was in a defensive posture and warned of a possible—I underscore "possible"—surprise attack?

INGLIS: In my opinion, it would.

DANFORTH: Now, Admiral Inglis, could you tell us just how long it took for the Navy's guns to gêt into action?

INGLIS: Yes, ready antiaircraft batteries opened fire immediately and within an average estimated time of under five minutes practically all battleship antiaircraft batteries were firing; cruisers were firing all antiaircraft batteries within an average time of four minutes; and destroyers, though opening up with machine guns almost immediately, averaged seven minutes in bringing all antiaircraft guns into action.

DANFORTH: So, even though the attack was a complete surprise, all batteries were firing within seven minutes after it began?

INGLIS: That is correct.

DANFORTH: Thank you, Admiral. I have no further questions.

PROCTOR indicates he has no questions

COURTNEY: You will not converse with anyone outside this courtroom concerning your testimony today.

INGLIS: Yes, sir.

COURTNEY: You are excused.

EXIT: INGLIS departs.

PROCTOR: Call Admiral Bellinger.

ENTER Admiral Bellinger, medium height, trim, athletic, handsome man; raises his right hand.

COURTNEY: You do solemnly swear that the testimony you are about to give will be the truth, the whole truth, and nothing but the truth. So help you God.

BELLINGER: I do.

Takes the witness chair.

PROCTOR: Admiral, will you state your name and length of time you have been in the Navy?

BELLINGER: Patrick Nelson Lynch Bellinger. I entered the Naval Academy in June 1903.

PROCTOR: Please state briefly your duties as of December 7, 1941.

BELLINGER: Commander, Hawaiian Based Patrol Wings and Commander, Patrol Wing 2. Included in the larger command were the patrol squadrons and aircraft tenders attached to Patrol Wings 1 and 2.

PROCTOR: Now, then, Admiral, did you in the course of your duties participate in the preparation of an air-defense plan for the Hawaiian Islands?

BELLINGER: About March 1, 1941, the Commander-in-Chief, Pacific Fleet, Admiral Kimmel, directed me to report to the Commandant, Fourteen Naval District, in connection with the preparation of an air-defense plan in conjunction with the Commanding General, Hawaiian Air Force. I proceeded with the assigned task, working directly with General Martin.

PROCTOR: You were the same Admiral Bellinger who prepared or aided in preparing the so-called Martin-Bellinger report, were you not?

BELLINGER: Yes, sir.

PROCTOR: Was that submitted to Admiral Kimmel?

BELLINGER: Yes, sir; copies went to him.

PROCTOR: And he approved it?

BELLINGER: Yes, sir.

PROCTOR: What was done with your report?

BELLINGER: Our study showed that for a commander to be reasonably sure that no hostile aircraft carrier could reach a spot 250 miles away and launch an attack without prior detection, would have required an effective daily search through 360 degrees to a distance of at least 800 miles. Assuming a 25-mile radius of visibility this would have required a daily 16-1/2-hour flight of 50 PBY-5 planes. This, in turn, would have necessitated a force of not less than 150 patrol planes, adequate spare parts, and ample well-trained personnel.

PROCTOR: Did Admiral Kimmel have the material to carry that plan into effect?

BELLINGER: Not in the complete state; no sir. We had 81 patrol planes in the whole Hawaiian area, including Midway. Of the 81 planes, 12 were conducting operations at Midway, 3 planes armed with gun and depth charges were engaged in the morning security patrol of fleet operating areas, 4 planes were conducting intertype tactics with submarines. Of the remaining 62 planes, 2 were on 15-minute notice, 8 were on 30-minute notice for operations, 9 were undergoing repairs, 43 were on 4-hour notice.

PROCTOR: Admiral, how many planes did the Navy have at Oahu on December 6, approximately?

BELLINGER: In accordance with my figures there were 48 patrol planes. There were no other planes that were available for long-distance search. The 8 Army B-17s reported to be were for bombardment. They did not report for any long-distance search.

PROCTOR: Then that would make a total of planes that you had, and Army B-17s, of 54?

BELLINGER: Fifty-seven.

PROCTOR: And were you yourself, with the planes that were available to you, making any long-distance patrols prior to December 7?

BELLINGER: Not for security purposes, no.

PROCTOR: For any purpose?

BELLINGER: Before December 7, the answer is no.

PROCTOR: When you arrived in Hawaii, did you expect war?

BELLINGER: Yes, sir.

PROCTOR: And that plan which you developed, was in effect a chart of exactly what happened at Pearl Harbor of December 7, 1941, with the exception of a few details; that is right, isn't it?

BELLINGER: Yes, sir.

PROCTOR: All right. Assuming that Japan decided to initiate the war by an air attack on the Pacific Fleet at Pearl Harbor, then would you assume the most likely way they would come would be from the northwest?

BELLINGER: Yes, I thought that would give them the most chances.

PROCTOR: I see. Now, as you have indicated in your previous answers, that sector was not covered by long-distance patrol or reconnaissance on the 6th of December?

BELLINGER: No.

PROCTOR: Can you give the reason for feeling that the north was the most dangerous sector?

BELLINGER: The question was where the Japanese were going to come from. It was a vital proposition to an aircraft carrier, in connection with the operation of planes. The carrier must head into the wind, and it must get up enough speed in order to have a sufficient force of wind over the deck. So, the direction of the wind controls the direction of movement of the carrier; and I don't believe an attack of the kind that was made on Pearl Harbor where surprise was expected to be a major affair, or where they felt there might be considerable jeopardy, would take place in a direction wherein the carrier had to take on her planes while heading toward the island.

PROCTOR: So if the prevailing wind is down from the north toward Oahu, then the best opportunity they have to get away is when the carriers are headed away from Oahu and the planes can be recaptured by the carrier heading right into the wind?

BELLINGER: Yes, sir.

PROCTOR: Is that right?

BELLINGER: Yes, sir.

PROCTOR: Admiral, do you believe there could have been reconnaissance if the command had been issued to have it?

BELLINGER: Yes, sir. With the planes we had there could have been reconnaissance.

PROCTOR: Am I correct in the assumption that you had sufficient planes at Pearl Harbor on December 7, and prior thereto, for a period of at least a week, to have enabled you to conduct long-range reconnaissance to the north for a period of a week?

BELLINGER: I would say "yes" to that question.

PROCTOR: You are of the opinion that with the patrol planes that were available it could have been carried on for at least a week?

BELLINGER: I think it could have, yes, sir.

PROCTOR: And effectively covered the arc from which you, as Air Force commander, at all times believed an air attack on Hawaii would come. Do I understand it to be your testimony?

BELLINGER: It could have covered that particular arc; yes, sir.

PROCTOR: Narrowing the matter down, if I interpret your testimony correctly—and if I am in error you can challenge me, Admiral—the failure to conduct a long-range reconnaissance which was, under the circumstances existent on December 7 at Pearl Harbor, practically the only way in which an attacking force of aircraft carriers could be discovered, rested entirely with the Commander-in-Chief and his staff, and until an order came from the Commander-in-Chief you would not, as a task force commander, control the planes to effect such reconnaissance, is that correct?

BELLINGER: That is correct.

PROCTOR: That is all.

PROCTOR returns to his desk. DANFORTH approaches the podium.

DANFORTH: Good afternoon, Admiral.

BELLINGER: Good afternoon, sir.

DANFORTH: My name is Charles Danforth. I am counsel for Admiral Kimmel. There are just a few questions I would like to ask about your testimony which you have just given.

BELLINGER: Yes, sir.

DANFORTH: Admiral, it is just a little bit difficult for me to understand, after such a remarkable report was drawn up in contemplation of a surprise attack, that everybody was surprised by the attack. I wonder if you can throw any light on it?

BELLINGER: As to why we were surprised?

DANFORTH: Yes.

BELLINGER: Well, we were at peace on December 6.

DANFORTH: I appreciate that. But, nevertheless, the Navy and Army were out in the Pacific, and you had drawn this plan, and it is a little difficult for me to understand just why there was not more confidence on the part of the Navy that there would be a possibility of an air attack on Pearl Harbor?

BELLINGER: Our report was not an estimate of the strategy that the Japanese would employ in starting this war. In other words, if they were going to strike Oahu, this is the estimate of how it would be done.

DANFORTH: If they were going to strike?

BELLINGER: If they were going to strike!

DANFORTH: Now, Admiral, realistically, you did not have 57 planes available for continuous long-distance patrol, did you? Some of those planes were earmarked for Wake Island, weren't they?

BELLINGER: Yes, sir.

DANFORTH: Admiral, how many squadrons of planes was Wake in a position to take care of on the week prior to December 7?

BELLINGER: Two squadrons could have operated from there for a short time.

DANFORTH: How many planes are there in a squadron?

BELLINGER: Twelve.

DANFORTH: Now, that would leave you, subtracting

24 from 57, with 33 planes at Pearl Harbor suitable for long-range patrol. You stated there were 57 in all. Deducting 24, that, under my arithmetic, would be 33, including the Army planes?

BELLINGER: Yes, sir.

DANFORTH: Now, all you had to do to get the Army planes was to ask for them, wasn't it?

BELLINGER: I never found it exactly that way.

DANFORTH: Have you any doubt today, Admiral, that if you had asked for those 8 B-17s to use in long-range reconnaissance out of Pearl Harbor you would have had any difficulty in getting them?

BELLINGER: If I asked for the B-17s entirely from information I had which was not concurred in by the Army, I would not have gotten them.

DANFORTH: In other words if you concluded that you wanted to initiate a long-distance patrol out of Pearl Harbor on the morning of December 6, you would have first had to persuade the Army that you were exercising good judgment in planning that patrol, and if they agreed with you, then they would let you have the planes?

BELLINGER: If they had them, yes.

DANFORTH: Well, did they have them?

BELLINGER: Yes, but they said they were for bombardment.

DANFORTH: Now it is my understanding, Admiral, that in flying long-distance reconnaissance, it isn't possible, as a practical matter, to operate the same crew and the same ship oftener than once in three days; is that right?

BELLINGER: That is correct for the crew, and practically correct for the ship.

DANFORTH: But the plane and crew could be used once every three days?

BELLINGER: That is correct.

DANFORTH: And if you had 33 long-distance patrol planes available on the 5th, 6th, and 7th of December, 11 of them could have been used for long-distance search.

BELLINGER: That is correct.

DANFORTH: And if each plane covered 8 degrees that would be an 88 degree search, wouldn't it?

BELLINGER: Correct.

DANFORTH: And the 11 planes could have given a first-class proper military scout of the entire northwest sector out of Oahu, isn't that correct?

BELLINGER: That is correct.

DANFORTH: And the search could have been continued, an echelon of 11 planes, for several weeks, couldn't it?

BELLINGER: Now we are talking about something that is a variable quantity. I would say that they could have been kept up, with a slight reduction maybe in the 11 per day, for about two weeks. It is a question of spare parts to replace the parts that are vital in a plane to keep the plane in commission. The new planes came out there with practically no spare parts to keep them operating. If there are no spare parts, the plane stays on the beach.

DANFORTH: Now isn't it true that your plan with General Martin covered a 360-degree reconnaissance?

BELLINGER: Yes, sir. 360 degrees on an island is the only way you can make sure that there is not a force coming in.

DANFORTH: Did you have any war plan that called for anything less, on a long-distance reconnaissance, than 360 degrees, the entire circle?

BELLINGER: Why certainly, the operating plan called for planes as they were available.

DANFORTH: Now, do I understand your testimony

to be—and you may correct me if I am in error—that the most dangerous sector, the greatest possibility of a successful air attack, lay in an attack coming from the north because of the prevailing wind conditions, is that right?

BELLINGER: That is practically correct; yes, sir.

DANFORTH: Did you so state in your report?

BELLINGER: No, sir, that is not in that report.

DANFORTH: Are you telling us that this report prepared by you and General Martin for the air defense of Hawaii, this report presented to and approved by Admiral Kimmel, this report contained no reference, suggestion, or warning as to the most likely direction of an attack being from the north or northwest?

BELLINGER: That is correct, sir.

DANFORTH: Did you have it within your power to make a recommendation to Admiral Kimmel that long-distance reconnaissance be used?

BELLINGER: Yes, sir. I could have recommended it.

DANFORTH: Did you ever make such a recommendation?

BELLINGER: I did not.

DANFORTH: Why not?

BELLINGER: We had no reason to expect such an attack, and the better practice was to conserve our very limited aircraft.

DANFORTH: Thank you, sir. No further questions.

DANFORTH returns to his desk. PROCTOR approaches the podium.

PROCTOR: Admiral, do you recall that in 1940, when Admiral Richardson, who was Admiral Kimmel's predecessor, was in command, he had naval planes on reconnaissance some six weeks?

BELLINGER: Yes; I remember that.

PROCTOR: Were you out there at that time?

BELLINGER: Yes, sir; part of the time.

PROCTOR: Well, then, if Admiral Richardson could do it, why couldn't Admiral Kimmel?

BELLINGER: I think I can answer that. In the first place, Admiral's Richardson's patrol ran out only to 300 miles. Moreover, the reconnaissance covered only the southwest sector towards the Marshall Islands where it was generally believed an attack would come from. . And second, I kept Admiral Kimmel very well informed as to the status of our aircraft. We were trying to get our planes replaced with new planes as quickly as possible.

PROCTOR: Assuming that you had been the commander out there and that you knew war was imminent, and you received a war-warning message, would that have made any difference in respect to using these planes for reconnaissance work?

BELLINGER: God only knows what I would have done. But I can say this, that I was very much surprised when I heard that there had been a message.

PROCTOR: Well, I was just coming to that. You were never confronted with the problem because you weren't taken into the confidence of those in command; isn't that right?

BELLINGER: In general, yes, sir.

PROCTOR: I have nothing further.

PROCTOR returns to desk. DANFORTH rises and speaks from desk.

DANFORTH: Now, according to War Plan 46, the patrol planes that the Navy had at Oahu were necessary for use of the fleet if the fleet should initiate an offensive operation out of the Pearl Harbor base, were they not?

BELLINGER: Yes, sir. They were primarily for the fleet use.

DANFORTH: And to the extent that the planes were used up, worn out, or grounded for lack of spare parts they would not have been available to the fleet for offensive operations; is that correct?

BELLINGER: Yes sir.

DANFORTH: Nothing further.

COURTNEY: You will not converse with anyone outside this courtroom concerning your testimony today. You are excused.

EXIT

PROCTOR: Call Admiral Turner.

ENTER Admiral Turner, a bullet-headed, pugnacious, arrogant man with outthrust jaw and steely eyes, raises his hand to be sworn.

COURTNEY: You do solemnly swear that the evidence you shall give in this court shall be the truth, the whole truth, and nothing but the truth. So help you God.

TURNER: I do.

Takes the witness chair.

PROCTOR: Will you state your name, present rank, Admiral, and station?

TURNER: My rank is Vice Admiral. My name is Richmond Kelly Turner. I am in command of the Amphibious Forces, Pacific Fleet.

PROCTOR: You were Chief of the War Plans Division in the Office of Naval Operations at one time, were you not?

TURNER: Yes, sir, from October 24, 1940, until June 13, 1942.

PROCTOR: Admiral Turner, I desire to commend you very highly on your splendid war record. I understood you to indicate that you were engaged in some of the greatest battles in the Pacific area. Is that correct?

TURNER: Yes, sir. Thank you.

PROCTOR: Will you state, Admiral, what were the functions of the War Plans Division, and War Plans Director in 1941 when you were there?

TURNER: May I quote from the pamphlet which I turned over to the Court?

PROCTOR: That is EXHIBIT 13, "Organization of the Office of Chief of Naval Operations, October 23, 1940," which relates to the War Plans Division. You may proceed.

TURNER: (Reading:)

(1) Development of policies and projects in support of war plans.

(2) Collaboration with the War Department in preparation of current plans for joint action of the Army and Navy, and in the solution of current problems.
(3) Collaboration with other Government departments on policies and projects affecting national defense.
(4) Study of subjects referred to the War Plans Division by the Chief of Naval Operations.
(5) Action in advisory capacity in current administrative matters referred to the War Plans Division.

PROCTOR: Admiral, there is one phase of your work that especially interests me, and that is the line of demarcation between the Office of Naval Intelligence, and the Office of War Plans, on the subject of evaluating intelligence information and disseminating it to the field commanders.

TURNER: In the Navy, it is the function of the War Plans Division to make and keep current the estimate as to the enemy, as well as to our own probable future actions.

At the time I came into office, estimates as to probable actions by foreign powers were going from the Office of Naval Intelligence to the Chief of Naval Operations and not routed by me...giving estimates as to what was going to happen. I was shown some of these by the Chief of Naval Operations and I disagreed with them very much.

So I talked to the Chief of Naval Intelligence and told him that when they prepared any evaluations as to strategic matters, they should route them through my office in advance so I could make a comment on them because that was my function, to give strategic advice.

PROCTOR: Let's get down to a specific case here, where on November 27, 1941, what was called a "war warning" was sent out to the commander of the Pacific Fleet at Hawaii which warned him that diplomatic relations had been broken, or words to that effect, that a hostile attack might be expected by the Japanese in any direction at any time, and so on. Now, was it your function to have any part in the drafting of that kind of document?

TURNER: I drew that document up. That was my conception and the conception of the Chief of Naval Operations and Assistant Chief. That was exactly the type of thing the War Plans was responsible for preparing.

PROCTOR: Admiral, that dispatch has been admitted as EXHIBIT 5. Would you be so kind as to read it into the record?

TURNER: (Reading:) THIS DESPATCH IS TO BE CONSIDERED A WAR WARNING [STOP] NEGOTIATIONS WITH JAPAN LOOKING TOWARD STABILIZATION OF CONDITIONS IN THE PACIFIC HAVE CEASED AND AN AGGRESSIVE MOVE BY JAPAN IS EXPECTED IN THE NEXT FEW DAYS [STOP] THE NUMBER AND EQUIPMENT OF JAPANESE TROOPS AND THE ORGANIZATION OF NAVAL FORCES INDICATES AN AMPHIBIOUS EXPEDITION AGAINST EITHER THE PHILIPPINES THAI OR KRA PENINSULA OR POSSIBLY TOWARD BORNEO. EXECUTE AN APPROPRIATE

DEFENSIVE DEPLOYMENT PREPARATORY TO CARRYING OUT THE TASKS ASSIGNED IN WPL [war plan] 46 [STOP] INFORM DISTRICT AND ARMY AUTHORITIES [STOP] A SIMILAR WARNING IS BEING SENT BY WAR DEPARTMENT [STOP] SPENAVO INFORM BRITISH [STOP] CONTINENTAL DISTRICTS GUAM AND SAMOA DIRECTED TO TAKE APPROPRIATE MEASURES AGAINST SABOTAGE [STOP].

PROCTOR: Now, here is a message that says, *"This is a war warning."* It says that *"...an aggressive move by Japan is expected within the next few days."* What was your reason for that statement?

TURNER: The number of messages and length of messages in the Japanese Fleet had been unusually high. Suddenly somewhere around the 25th or 26th of November the traffic level dropped very markedly and the Japanese changed their code, and changed their calls.

Well, that was very significant and that very important operations were contemplated, and it was probable that nearly the entire Japanese Fleet had put to sea.

Roughly, I thought the chances were about 50-50 that we would get a heavy raid in Hawaii.

PROCTOR: Well, you had an impression then, when you heard the reports relating to the location of all these carriers and a couple of battleships, you had in mind that there was a 50-50 chance that Hawaii would be attacked?

TURNER: Yes, sir; at least.

PROCTOR: So, it was your opinion that an attack on Pearl Harbor was imminent?

TURNER: Probable.

PROCTOR: So you drafted the war warning message of November 27, 1941, to Admiral Kimmel?

TURNER: Yes, sir.

PROCTOR: And is it your conviction if Admiral Kimmel had carried out the order drafted by you and sent to him on November 27, 1941, that an attack by Japan on Pearl Harbor could have been defeated or the effects greatly reduced?

TURNER: Yes, sir, to have inflicted very serious damage on the Japanese Fleet.

PROCTOR: Returning to your dispatch, it states: *"The number and equipment of Japanese troops and the organization of naval task forces indicates an amphibious expedition against either the Philippines, Thai or Kra Peninsula or possibly Borneo."* Why did you put in a reference to the Philippines, Thai, or Kra, or Borneo?

TURNER: We wanted to emphasize the fact that this was a very important major effort. The message tells Admiral Kimmel to execute an appropriate defensive deployment. That is perfectly specific and entirely clear.

PROCTOR: Well, coming to the next sentence in your message, it says: *"Execute an appropriate defensive deployment preparatory to carrying out the tasks assigned in WPL-46."* What is meant by that? Specifically, what is meant by "appropriate defensive deployment?"

TURNER: A "deployment" is a spreading out of forces. A naval deployment means to spread out and make ready for hostilities. Instead of being concentrated in one place, or instead of being off in some distant region holding exercises and drills, it meant that the forces under the command of the Commander-in-Chief of the Pacific Fleet could take station for the most probable attack against them or against the Hawaiian Islands.

PROCTOR: War Plan 46 is a voluminous document, but can you briefly state to this court just what the operation in general called for, so we may better understand what the preparatory deployment referred to in your warning message would be?

TURNER: (Reading:) *"Task H: Protect the territory of the Associated powers in the Pacific area and prevent the expansion of enemy military power into the Western Hemisphere by destroying hostile expeditions and by supporting land and air forces in denying the use of land positions in that hemisphere."* That is the major defensive task of the Pacific Fleet.

PROCTOR: And does that include Hawaii?

TURNER: Yes sir. The plan says, *"protect the territory of Associated Powers,"* and we are defined as one of the associated powers.

PROCTOR: Then when you ordered him to "Execute an appropriate defensive deployment preparatory to carrying our the tasks assigned in WPL 46," did you mean the commander of the Pacific Fleet should take preparatory deployment measures for those operations you just read us?

TURNER: It says, *"Execute an appropriate defensive deployment."*

PROCTOR: Defensive?

TURNER: Yes.

PROCTOR: I believe you stated that in your opinion his fleet should not have been concentrated in Pearl Harbor on that Sunday morning, December 7, 1941?

TURNER: I did not say that in those words. I said the business of the fleet was to be so deployed as best to carry out a defense of the region and to prepare to carry out the other tasks of the war plan. Personally, I would have had them at sea, except those under repair.

PROCTOR: You thought then that the ships and naval forces should have been at sea on that Sunday morning, December 7, 1941?

TURNER: Yes, sir.

PROCTOR: And you certainly do not think that they should have been tied up two and two in the harbor?

TURNER: No, sir. I, myself, feel that local safety could have been better obtained if the fleet had been a sea.

PROCTOR: Well, was it solely within the discretion and jurisdiction of the Commander-in-Chief of the Pacific Fleet, Admiral Kimmel, as to whether his ships were all in Pearl Harbor, as they appeared on December 7, 1941, or were out at sea?

TURNER: It was within his province entirely.

PROCTOR: And he was the one who made that decision as to just what he did with his fleet and how he handled it, and used it, rather than somebody in Washington?

TURNER: Yes, sir.

PROCTOR: Now, with reference the order to "Execute an appropriate defensive deployment," in your opinion, Admiral, did Admiral Kimmel comply with that part of this order?

TURNER: He did not, in my opinion.

PROCTOR: If he had complied with that part of this order, do you think the disastrous effects suffered by the Pacific Fleet at Pearl Harbor on December 7, 1941, would not have occurred or would have been materially reduced?

TURNER: I think they would have been materially reduced and I believe there would have been a good chance of inflicting considerable damage on the Japanese Fleet.

PROCTOR: I want to turn now to the question of air reconnaissance. From your knowledge, how much air reconnaissance did Admiral Kimmel have in the air on the 6th day of December 1941, the day before the attack?

TURNER: None.

PROCTOR: Would you say that you regarded the failure of any reconnaissance of any character on the 6th, the day before the attack, that the failure to have any sort of reconnaissance at Pearl Harbor on the 6th of December, was a violation of the command order you had sent out on the 27th?

TURNER: It was a violation of it.

PROCTOR: Now, you were kept fully advised and informed as to the developments of all diplomatic relations between this country and Japan, were you?

TURNER: I was kept advised and I think I had fully adequate information.

PROCTOR: Did you reach the conclusion that war with Japan was inevitable?

TURNER: Yes, sir.

PROCTOR: When did you reach that conclusion?

TURNER: June and July of 1941.

PROCTOR: During June and July of 1941, you became convinced that war, and you were certain that war between the United States and Japan would occur?

TURNER: Within the next few months.

PROCTOR: Did you at any time think an attack would be made on Pearl Harbor?

TURNER: Yes, sir. I thought there was always a strong possibility and even a probability that a raid on Hawaii would precede any declaration of war and would be simultaneous with other operations. I always believed that.

PROCTOR: And the raid made by Japan on Pearl Harbor December 7, 1941, could have been defeated or the effect of that raid greatly reduced if proper measures had been taken by the local commander?

TURNER: That is my belief.

PROCTOR: Now, the message of November 27, 1941, which was drafted by you, and sent by the Chief of Naval Operations, the beginning of that message reads: *"This dispatch is to be considered a war warning."* Could there be any question about the interpretation of those words who was in command of a fleet anywhere in the Pacific or otherwise?

TURNER: I do not see now, and I did not see then, that there was any possibility of misinterpreting that sentence.

PROCTOR: If Admiral Kimmel had complied with this message, would his command have been properly alerted? In other words, was this message of November 27 to him sufficient to require the proper alert of his command?

TURNER: I believe it was.

PROCTOR: And if he had complied with this message his command would have been on the proper alert?

TURNER: I believe so.

PROCTOR: Now, after all these messages have gone forward advising Admiral Kimmel of the situation between these two nations, as the Chief of Naval Operations saw them, what he did with the fleet upon these instructions was his own responsibility under Navy orders?

TURNER: That is correct.

PROCTOR: No further questions.

PROCTOR addresses the Court.

PROCTOR: If the Court please, Admiral Turner has received orders requiring his immediate presence elsewhere. I am sorry but I cannot be more specific, but I represent to the court that it is necessary that he be excused, albeit temporarily, and I ask that his cross-examination be deferred until such time as exigencies allow.

DANFORTH: Counsel has apprised me of the situation, your Honor, and the defense has no objection so long, of course, as the trial is not ended without the cross-examination of Admiral Turner.

COURTNEY: Very well, without objection, Admiral Turner, you are not to discuss your testimony with anyone other than counsel.

EXIT

PROCTOR: The prosecution rests, subject to the cross-examination of Admiral Turner.

COURTNEY: I think this is a good spot to take a 10-minute recess.

Stage darkens. House lights come up

* * *

ACT II: The Defense

ORDERLY: All rise!

COURTNEY: Court is in session. Be seated, please.

All sit.

COURTNEY: Is the Defense ready to proceed?

DANFORTH: We are, your honor.

COURTNEY: You may call your first witness.

DANFORTH: Call Admiral Wilkinson.

ENTER Admiral Wilkinson, a tall, somewhat fleshy, genial man. He raises his right hand.

COURTNEY: You do solemnly swear that the evidence you shall give in this court shall be the truth, the whole truth, and nothing but the truth. So help you God.

WILKINSON: I do.

Takes the witness chair

DANFORTH: Admiral, will you please state your name, your rank, and present duty for the record, please, sir?

WILKINSON: Theodore Stark Wilkinson, Vice Admiral, U.S. Navy, recently commander of the Third Amphibious Force of the Pacific Fleet, and now awaiting assignment by the Navy Department for duty.

DANFORTH: During what period of time were you Director of Naval Intelligence?

WILKINSON: From October the 15th, 1941, until, as I recall, July the 20th, 1942.

DANFORTH: How long have you been in the Navy, Admiral?

WILKINSON: Forty-and-a-half years.

DANFORTH: What were some of the functions and responsibilities of Naval Intelligence?

WILKINSON: The duties of the office as a whole and of the foreign branch in particular and of each geographic section was to collect, evaluate and forward to interested agencies intelligence received from abroad or picked up from newspapers or otherwise with relation to the several foreign countries under each geographic section. The evaluation will consist of considering the source, considering the reliability of the information and its consistency with other proven information.

DANFORTH: Did the Office of Naval Intelligence keep track of the movements of the Japanese and other potential enemy nation vessels?

WILKINSON: Very definitely.

DANFORTH: Admiral, let me hand you what has been marked as EXHIBIT 14, which is a three-sheet mimeographed document entitled "Intelligence Division (OP-16) Duties." Does that document correctly summarize the duties of the Intelligence Division as it was set up and operating immediately prior to Pearl Harbor?

WILKINSON: Yes, sir.

DANFORTH: I ask you, Admiral, to read duties (1) and (2) of the Foreign Intelligence Branch.

WILKINSON: (Reading)

(1) Secure all classes of pertinent information concerning foreign countries, especially that affect-

ing naval and maritime matters, with particular attention to the strength, disposition and probable intentions of foreign naval forces.

(2) Evaluate the information collected and disseminate as advisable.

DANFORTH: So, as I understand it, under items (1) and (2), it is clear that your duty was to secure information concerning the disposition and probable intentions of foreign naval forces, evaluate that information, and disseminate it, was it not?

WILKINSON: No, sir. With respect to accuracy, very definitely. With respect to the determination of probable intentions, it was not.

DANFORTH: But you did have, as one of your functions, the responsibility of determining what the probable intentions of the foreign naval forces would be?

WILKINSON: No. Although that is specifically stated in the Exhibit, I was advised by my predecessor that he had been told by the Chief of Naval Operations, the Assistant Chief, and the Director of War Plans, that the Office of Naval Intelligence would not prepare the estimate of probable intentions of the enemy, but that War Plans, under Admiral Turner, would assume that duty.

DANFORTH: The duties that I have just introduced as EXHIBIT 14, were established by the order of the Chief of Naval Operations on October 23, 1940, were they not?

WILKINSON: I believe so.

DANFORTH: Do you know of any formal written amendment of those duties, Admiral?

WILKINSON: No, sir.

DANFORTH: It was not your duty to determine the probable intentions of the enemy?

WILKINSON: I did not so understand.

DANFORTH: In other words, where you reached a situation which led you to feel that the information disseminated might approach the area of a directive, you felt you were required to consult Admiral Turner in War Plans?

WILKINSON: Exactly.

DANFORTH: Let me hand you what has been marked EXHIBIT 15, and ask if you can identify it?

WILKINSON: Yes, it is a memo from the CNO to the Director of Naval Intelligence, dated December 12, 1940.

DANFORTH: Going down to paragraph 3, would you please read that, Admiral?

WILKINSON: (Reading:) *It is desired that no information be included pertaining to the United States,*

British or Dutch military on naval dispositions and strengths, nor should reference be made to United Sates war plans or secret diplomatic conversations. Signed H.R. Stark.

DANFORTH: What did you understand to be the import of the memo?

WILKINSON: Because of the extreme security attached to our code-breaking activities, these fortnightly summaries should not contain information concerning secret diplomatic conversations.

DANFORTH: Do you know whether Admiral Kimmel had ever been advised that you were not going to submit to him information concerning secret diplomatic conversations?

WILKINSON: I do not know.

DANFORTH: Had you ever heard that Admiral Kimmel had requested such information be sent to him?

WILKINSON: No, sir. I now know, but I did not know then.

DANFORTH: What do you mean, you now know?

WILKINSON: I have recently seen a transcript of a letter from Admiral Kimmel requesting that he be kept advised of diplomatic activities.

DANFORTH: You are referring to Admiral Kimmel's

request to Admiral Stark that he be advised concerning diplomatic matters?

WILKINSON: Yes, sir. I did not know of it then, and only recently in connection with this trial have I seen it.

DANFORTH: I have in my hand, Admiral, a letter of February 18, 1941, addressed to Admiral Stark by Admiral Kimmel, marked EXHIBIT 8. I will simply read the pertinent portions relating to this matter of information. (Reading:)

I have recently been told by an officer fresh from Washington that ONI considers it the function of War Plans to furnish the Commander-in-Chief with information of a secret nature. I have heard also that War Plans considers the responsibility for furnishing the same type of information to be that of ONI. I do not know that we have missed anything, but if there is any doubt as to whose responsibility it is to keep the Commander-in-Chief fully informed with pertinent reports on subjects that should be of interest to the Fleet, will you kindly fix that responsibility so that there will be no misunderstanding?

To that letter there is a reply from Admiral Stark dated March 22, 1941, marked EXHIBIT 16, I will read the portion relating to the postscript I have just read from Admiral Kimmel's letter.

With reference to your postscript... Kirk informs me that ONI is fully aware of its responsibility in keeping you adequately informed....

I also find a memorandum for the Chief of Naval Operations, dated March 11, 1941, signed by A.G. Kirk, from the Office of Naval Intelligence, marked EXHIBIT 17, which is apparently the basis for Admiral Stark's answer to the postscript of Admiral Kimmel's letter, in which is stated:

4. The Division of Naval Intelligence is fully aware that it is the responsibility of this division to keep the Commander-in-Chief, Pacific Fleet, adequately informed concerning foreign nations, activities of these nations, and disloyal elements within the United States.

Now, with those letters in mind, I will ask you, first, the A.G. Kirk who signed the memorandum of March 11, 1941, was then Director of Naval Intelligence?

WILKINSON: Yes, sir.

DANFORTH: That is the position you held?

WILKINSON: I relieved him directly.

DANFORTH: When you became Chief of Naval Intelligence, did Admiral Kirk inform you of the correspondence between Admiral Stark and Admiral Kimmel, and of his memorandum which I just read to you?.

WILKINSON: No. I will explain further that it would obviously be undesirable for me to send out information which on its receipt would cause the Commander-in-Chief, Pacific Fleet, to take such action as would be in conflict with the action which was desired by the responsible officer in the Department for War Plans.

DANFORTH: That officer would be Admiral Turner?

WILKINSON: Yes.

DANFORTH: And still Admiral Kirk issues a memorandum in which he says that it is his responsibility, and we have also in the record that Admiral Stark says it was the responsibility of ONI.

WILKINSON: Yes, sir.

DANFORTH: That is pretty definite, isn't it?

WILKINSON: All right.

DANFORTH: Then I will ask you, Admiral Wilkinson, why you didn't transmit the information that was contained in the Japanese intercepts to Admiral Kimmel, Commander-in-Chief of the Pacific Fleet, when the information pointed directly to Hawaii?

WILKINSON: That information was little more than what they had through their own intelligence agencies.

DANFORTH: Admiral Kimmel did not have access to a "Purple" machine that would decode Japanese diplomatic messages, did he?

WILKINSON: No, sir.

DANFORTH: My dear sir, don't you think you were assuming a tremendous responsibility in deciding in your mind what Admiral Kimmel knew?

WILKINSON: No, sir. I am not quite, as yet, in agreement with the fact I should have supplied it to him.

DANFORTH: And by withholding from him that information you denied him the opportunity to decide what importance should be attached to those messages in that way, didn't you, and you denied him the right to act in the light of what those messages conveyed, didn't you?

WILKINSON: Yes, sir.

DANFORTH: No further questions. *(To PROCTOR:)* You may examine.

Returns to desk. PROCTOR approaches podium.

PROCTOR: Admiral, I believe in your testimony, you mentioned the general security attached to code-breaking operations. Was that a matter of high concern to the Chief of Naval Operations?

WILKINSON: Yes, sir.

PROCTOR: Now, if the contents of intercepted Japanese dispatches were sent directly to the field, there would be a risk that they might be intercepted or compromised by the enemy, is that not correct?

WILKINSON: Yes, sir.

PROCTOR: Thank you, Admiral. No further questions.

Sits

DANFORTH: Now, I believe that you explained the discrepancies between the schedule of organization of 23 October 1940 and your conception of your duties by pointing out that you had received verbal orders that prohibited you from sending intelligence estimates of enemy's intentions to commanders in the field?

WILKINSON: Yes, sir.

DANFORTH: And who did you say gave you those verbal orders?

WILKINSON: I think I stated that I was officially informed by my predecessor as part of my relieving him that he had been directed by Admiral Stark to that effect in the presence of Admiral Turner.

DANFORTH: And you are still prepared to stand by this testimony?

WILKINSON: Yes, sir.

DANFORTH: No further questions.

Sits

COURTNEY: You will refrain from discussing with anyone outside this courtroom concerning your testimony today.

WILKINSON: Yes, sir.

COURTNEY: You are excused.

EXIT

DANFORTH: Call Admiral Leigh Noyes

ENTER Admiral Noyes, a diminutive, square-jawed man with receding hairline. He raises his right hand.

COURTNEY: You do solemnly swear that the evidence you shall give in this court shall be the truth, the whole truth, and nothing but the truth. So help you God.

NOYES: I do.

Takes the witness chair.

DANFORTH: Admiral Noyes, will you please state your full name, your rank, and present assignment.

NOYES: Leigh Noyes. Rear Admiral, U.S. Navy. President of the Board of Inspection and Survey.

DANFORTH: And what were your duties on the 7th of December 1941?

NOYES: I was Director of Naval Communications.

DANFORTH: At the time, the principal function of your office was the maintenance of the Navy's communication system, was it not?

NOYES: Yes, sir.

DANFORTH: Turning to the interception and decryption of the Japanese messages, we know from the testimony before this Court that the Navy was maintaining a system of monitoring stations for the interception of those messages. You were familiar, were you not, with that system?

NOYES: I was.

DANFORTH: Now in addition to the intercepting system of monitoring stations, did the Navy Department also maintain facilities in Washington and at Corregidor and Pearl Harbor for decrypting Japanese messages?

NOYES: Yes, sir.

DANFORTH: You were familiar with the assignments and facilities available at Pearl Harbor and at Corregidor, were you not?

NOYES: Yes, sir.

DANFORTH: Was it your understanding, prior to December 7, there were no facilities at Pearl Harbor for the decryption of Japanese messages in the "Purple" code?

NOYES: That is correct.

DANFORTH: Admiral Turner has testified before this court that it was his understanding there were facilities at Pearl Harbor which permitted the people at Pearl Harbor to read the Japanese diplomatic messages. Did Admiral Turner ever discuss the matter with you?

NOYES: I know the question. I think it has been stated by Admiral Turner that he discovered he was mistaken. He had confused traffic analysis with decryption.

DANFORTH: Now did you ever make any statements to Admiral Turner that Admiral Kimmel was able to read the translated or decrypted messages in "Purple" code at Pearl Harbor?

NOYES: Not to the best of my knowledge and belief.

DANFORTH: Do you think that he had the two types of information confused in his mind?

NOYES: That is merely my opinion.

DANFORTH: That is merely your opinion?

NOYES: Yes.

DANFORTH: Admiral, does the name "magic" mean anything to you?

NOYES: "Magic" is the name given to the decrypted Japanese purple code messages; "Purple" refers to a specific Japanese diplomatic code. We had several worries that the Japanese were finding out the fact that we were reading their code, and it caused us to be more careful about what we were doing.

DANFORTH: Therefore the term "magic" was used to refer to the messages, and "purple" to the code?

NOYES: In general, yes, sir. That was our way of disguising what we were doing. Often we used the terms interchangeably.

DANFORTH: Will you explain the purpose of the arrangement that was set up here, whereby "magic" applied only to the Philippines?

NOYES: This arrangement was set up in order to cut down on the amount of transmission to Washington and speed up the entire operation.

DANFORTH: So this was, in effect, an arrangement to keep the Army and Navy in the Philippines informed as to what each was doing in regard to the interception and decryption of Japanese diplomatic messages, but not Hawaii; is that correct?

NOYES: This plan could not have worked for Hawaii, because there was no machine available for Hawaii.

DANFORTH: But if there were advantages in making the information available in the Philippines with regard to "purple" traffic, might there not have been similar advantages in Hawaii arranging for exchange of information in connection with messages that were being handled and decrypted by the Army and Navy in Hawaii?

NOYES: In the first place, we did not have another machine.

DANFORTH: I realize that.

NOYES: And in the second place, our plan was to have Hawaii concentrate on the naval codes.

DANFORTH: Thank you, Admiral. I have no further questions.

DANFORTH returns to desk. PROCTOR rises and goes to podium

PROCTOR: Admiral, was there any deliberate effort to keep information from Hawaii?

NOYES: No, sir; not to my knowledge.

PROCTOR: And Hawaii had all the information you had?

NOYES: To the best of my knowledge and belief, it did.

PROCTOR: No further questions.

DANFORTH: (Rising in chair.) They didn't have "magic" did they?

NOYES: No, sir.

DANFORTH: And they didn't have the intercepted 14-part message, did they?

NOYES: No, sir.

DANFORTH: Thank you. No further questions.

COURTNEY: You are excused. You will refrain from conversing with anyone outside this courtroom concerning your testimony today.

NOYES: Yes, sir.

EXIT

DANFORTH: Call Captain Kramer

ENTER Captain Kramer, a smallish, narrow-faced man with pencil-thin mustache. He raises his right hand.

COURTNEY: You do solemnly swear that the evidence

you shall give in this court shall be the truth, the whole truth, and nothing but the truth. So help you God.

KRAMER: I do.

Takes the witness chair.

DANFORTH: Captain, will you give your name in full to the reporter?

KRAMER: Captain Alwin Dalton Kramer, United States Navy.

DANFORTH: How long have you been in the Navy?

KRAMER: Since 1925.

DANFORTH: What was your position in the months leading up to December 7, 1941?

KRAMER: I was Chief of the Translation Section, Department of the Navy.

DANFORTH: I want to show you a message marked EXHIBIT 18. Are you familiar with that?

KRAMER: I am, sir.

DANFORTH: Would you describe it?

KRAMER: It is the "pilot message" for delivery of an intercepted 14-part message from Tokyo to the Japanese Embassy in Washington.

DANFORTH: When did you first see that message?

KRAMER: I believe on Saturday evening, 6 December 1941. It was translated, as indicated, on the 6th of December.

DANFORTH: Yes. Now, was that message delivered to the Secretary of the Navy and the President on the evening of the 6th?

KRAMER: I am quite certain, sir, that that was included in the folder I delivered that night.

DANFORTH: Would you read the message?

KRAMER: (Reading:) *"From: Tokyo. To: Washington. December 6, 1941. #904. Re My #902. There is really no need to tell you this, but in preparation of the aide memoire be absolutely sure not to use a typist or other person. Be most extremely cautious in preserving secrecy."*

DANFORTH: Now, that message "In re my Number 902" referred to the long diplomatic reply to Secretary Hull's message of the 26th?

KRAMER: Yes, sir.

DANFORTH: What interpretation did you give this message that they were to use no typist, they were to deliver it personally themselves, and to "be most extremely cautious in preserving secrecy?".

I want you to consider at the same time you had a pilot message indicating that this #902 was to be delivered when a certain time was given to them in Washington.

KRAMER: I do not recollect precisely my reaction to this thing, sir. It was included, however, in the folders delivered that night with the first 13 parts of that note. I believe my reaction at the time was that the note itself was of a much more serious nature than previous notes forwarded to this country.

DANFORTH: You had read the 13 parts, had you?

KRAMER: Before I went to the White House, I had; yes, sir.

DANFORTH: What conclusion did you draw as to the status of diplomatic relations between the United States and Japan were concerned?

KRAMER: That they were probably at an end.

DANFORTH: Now, did you have a conversation with anyone at the White House that night?

KRAMER: A brief one; yes, sir, with one of the junior officers in the Situation Room.

DANFORTH: What was said?

KRAMER: The general tenor of our conversation was

to the effect that there was something of high importance in that pouch which the President should see as soon as possible.

DANFORTH: Admiral Beardall was the President's Naval Aide?

KRAMER: Yes, sir.

DANFORTH: Do you know where Admiral Beardall was that evening?

KRAMER: Admiral Beardall was at Admiral Wilkinson's home. I felt undoubtedly Admiral Beardall would check up later in the evening to see whether the President had yet received the message, presuming that if he had not, Admiral Beardall himself would then come down to the White House to see that he did see it.

DANFORTH: Have you ever learned as to whether or not Admiral Beardall did check up with the President as to whether or not he got that 13th part and this Number 904?

KRAMER: I only know, sir, that I informed Admiral Beardall when I arrived at Admiral Wilkinson's home . I do not know what further action Admiral Beardall took.

DANFORTH: Have you learned later?

KRAMER: No, sir.

DANFORTH: Now, whom did you call before you left the Navy Department?

KRAMER: I attempted to call Admiral Stark's home and Admiral Turner's home. I didn't succeed in reaching either one of those people. I called my own home, requested my wife to bring the car down to expedite delivery that night. I called Captain McCollum at his home in Alexandria. I called Secretary Knox's apartment at the Wardman Park Hotel. And after making all these calls, I then called Admiral Wilkinson to inform him of whom I had been able to contact and what I prepared to do in the way of delivery.

DANFORTH: At what time would you say you called their homes?

KRAMER: It was within a few minutes of nine o'clock.

DANFORTH: Now, did you know that the evaluation of these messages had been turned over to Admiral Turner's office and taken away from the Intelligence branch? Did you know that?

KRAMER: I was unfamiliar with that, sir, until these hearings commenced.

DANFORTH: You didn't know it then, when you called Admiral Turner?

KRAMER: On that particular point, yes, sir; that was my understanding.

DANFORTH: Then, as I understand it, from the testimony we have here now, that Admiral Turner's office had taken over the evaluation of these messages, his office was apparently not alerted for war on the night of the 6th because you couldn't reach him; is that correct?

KRAMER: I couldn't reach him; no, sir.

DANFORTH: And Admiral Stark, apparently his office was not alerted, because you were unable to reach him; is that correct?

KRAMER: I was unable to reach him; that is all I can say.

DANFORTH: All right. Then as I understand it now, Admiral Stark's office could not be reached. His home could not be reached. The next in line, Admiral Turner's office couldn't be reached, and his home couldn't be reached, and there were no other officers assigned to which these important messages could be delivered?

KRAMER: Yes, sir, there were.

DANFORTH: Who were the officers?

KRAMER: Admiral Wilkinson, the Director of Naval Intelligence.

DANFORTH: Then do I understand you conferred with Wilkinson and that it didn't reach anyone out of his office—and he didn't have the authority, as we have learned here, to evaluate these messages—they were to be delivered to War Plans for evaluation as far as the Navy was concerned, were they not?

KRAMER: I have stated I am unaware of what arrangements were made regarding evaluation. Admiral Wilkinson's instructions to me were to have this material ready to deliver promptly early the following morning as soon as Admiral Stark reached his office.

DANFORTH: Now, you went down to Wilkinson's home, did you not?

KRAMER: Admiral Wilkinson's home, yes, sir.

DANFORTH: And you found there what officers?

KRAMER: The naval aide to the President, Admiral Beardall, Admiral Wilkinson, and General Miles, head of Army Intelligence.

DANFORTH: Well, now, you really had Intelligence in one room, didn't you—top man in the Army, top man in the Navy, and top man in the White House?

KRAMER: Yes, sir; one room.

DANFORTH: And you had in a bag, in a brief case, a pilot message for delivery of a 14-part Japanese message, telling that there was going to be war sooner than anyone thought; is that correct?

KRAMER: That is correct, sir.

DANFORTH: Those gentlemen took the messages out of the bag and read them; is that correct?

KRAMER: That is correct; sir.

DANFORTH: How long were you in this room with these gentlemen?

KRAMER: I should say approximately one-half hour, except for the time I left the room to go out to my car where my wife was waiting.

DANFORTH: Now, I assume that you told them that the Secretary of the Navy was the only other man in the Navy, outside the President, that you had been able to reach about these messages?

KRAMER: Except for the fact that I informed Admiral Wilkinson that I had phoned Captain McCollum about them.

DANFORTH: Now, did you tell them that Secretary Knox had arranged a meeting for the following morning at 10 o'clock with the Secretary of War and the Secretary of State?

KRAMER: I did, sir.

DANFORTH: And what was their reply?

KRAMER: Admiral Wilkinson told me to be there on time, or something to that effect.

DANFORTH: Did he tell you it would not be necessary for you to try later to reach Stark?

KRAMER: My recollection is that I asked him, and I was not so instructed.

DANFORTH: What did he tell you?

KRAMER: As I previously stated, he specifically told me to have these ready for delivery to Admiral Stark as soon as he arrived in the office Sunday morning.

DANFORTH: What did Admiral Wilkinson say to you about delivery to Admiral Turner?

KRAMER: The same thing applies to Admiral Turner as to Admiral Stark.

DANFORTH: *(Holds up document.)* I read from EXHIBIT 19. *(Reading:) "Will the Ambassador please submit to the United States Government (if possible to the Secretary of State) our reply to the United States at 1:00 p.m. on the 7th, your time."*

So that made it so that there was to be a delivery to the United States, to the Secretary of State, on Sunday at one o'clock?

KRAMER: Yes, sir.

DANFORTH: Now, I will ask you when that message was received and decoded?

KRAMER: It was not received, or at least seen by me, until about the middle of Sunday morning.

DANFORTH: So you would say you delivered it to the White House at what time?

KRAMER: I should say it was between twenty and a quarter of 10.

DANFORTH: Twenty and a quarter of 10, is that right?

KRAMER: That is my recollection now, sir.

DANFORTH: Thank you, Captain. No further questions.

COURTNEY looks at PROCTOR, who half-rises at his desk, shakes his head.

COURTNEY: You are excused. You are admonished to refrain from discussing your testimony with any person outside this courtroom.

KRAMER: Yes, sir.

EXIT

DANFORTH: I call Captain Safford.

ENTER Captain Safford, a tall, slender, professo-

rial man with steel-gray hair. He raises his right hand.

COURTNEY: You do solemnly swear that the evidence you shall give in this court shall be the truth, the whole truth, and nothing but the truth. So help you God.

SAFFORD: I do.

Takes the witness chair.

DANFORTH: Captain, will you give your name, rank, and present duty station?

SAFFORD: Laurence Frye Safford, Captain, Assistant Director of Naval Intelligence for cryptographic research.

DANFORTH: What were your duties during the period of November and December 1941?

SAFFORD: I was in charge of the Navy Department Communication Intelligence Unit from May 1936 until February 15, 1942.

DANFORTH: What is meant by "communication intelligence?"

SAFFORD: By "communication intelligence," I mean the interception of the radio messages of enemy foreign nations and agents, their solution by cryptoanalytic processes.

DANFORTH: It is a fact, is it not, Captain that the Washington office had the most experienced personnel and was the most extensive office of that kind that we had in the world, was it not?

SAFFORD: It was the largest we had. I would say that the best we had, as far as experience and all-around skill, was at Pearl Harbor.

DANFORTH: Was there any division of activity assigned to these various stations, for instance, Washington, Pearl Harbor, and Corregidor, as to what character of work they should do, or were they doing all the same thing?

SAFFORD: That was highly specialized. Washington was responsible for handling Japanese diplomatic communications.

DANFORTH: Captain, you recall in a general way that there was an intercepted message which came into this country from Japan in 14 parts—first a 13-part message followed by an "execute" message?

SAFFORD: Yes, sir. Tokyo filed the first 13 parts as separate messages a few minute apart over a span of three or four hours, apparently, to finish encoding it. These 13 parts came in Saturday afternoon, December 6. Then they delayed about 12 hours before they filed the 14th part. It came in early Sunday morning.

DANFORTH: Why did you consider the 14-part message so important?

SAFFORD: The Japanese, for the first time in the whole series of negotiations, became very abusive in their language....

DANFORTH: And what conclusion did you draw?

SAFFORD: That they were breaking off diplomatic relations...and it was probably the last message we would ever receive from the Japanese government.

DANFORTH: That message came in on the "purple" machine, did it not?

SAFFORD: Yes, sir.

DANFORTH: Did Hawaii have "purple?"

SAFFORD: It did not.

DANFORTH: Do you know whether any part of the intercepted 14-part message had been sent to Hawaii? I am speaking of the 13 parts now.

SAFFORD: I know that none of it was ever sent to Hawaii.

DANFORTH: Captain, can you tell us the circumstances of how you received word of the surprise attack on Pearl Harbor?

SAFFORD: I left the office at the close of working hours, at 4:30 p.m. on Saturday, December 6. I stayed out late Saturday night. I was eating breakfast in my pajamas and bathrobe when I received a telephone call from the watch officer that the Japanese had attacked Hawaii. I realized that there had been a slip, and a bad slip, high up in the Navy Department.

DANFORTH: What was that last?

SAFFORD: That there was a slip in the Navy Department, high up.

DANFORTH: What was that slip?

PROCTOR: *(Rising)* Objection. Calls for a conclusion from the witness.

COURTNEY: Sustained.

DANFORTH: All right, Captain. At what time did you return to your office?

SAFFORD: At the beginning of working hours on Monday, which I believe was 8:00 a.m.

DANFORTH: And was your attention then called to anything relating to this 14-part message?

SAFFORD: I immediately called a conference with all of my heads of sub-sections. I called them to find out what had gone wrong and how the people had been surprised the way they had; first, to see if our section had been to blame in any other way, and second, to immediately start writing a full report of the circumstances as required by Navy regulations.

DANFORTH: Did you make any notes of this conference?

SAFFORD: Yes, sir.

DANFORTH: Do you have those notes with you?

SAFFORD: No, sir.

DANFORTH: Why not?

SAFFORD: Sometime within the week following Pearl Harbor, I and the other officers were called into conference in the office of the Director of Naval Communications; I am not certain whether Admiral Noyes presided or Captain Redmond, the Assistant Director.

DANFORTH: The meeting was called for what purpose?

SAFFORD: The meeting was called to discuss the attack on Pearl Harbor and the whispering campaign against Admiral Kimmel and Admiral Bloch which was then getting into full swing.

DANFORTH: What was the general tenor of that meeting, as best you can recall?

SAFFORD: The discussion in that meeting was that there was too much loose talk going around, that there would undoubtedly be an investigation later, and if we had written anything to destroy it immediately.

DANFORTH: Who gave you the order that you were to destroy anything, name those people?

SAFFORD: It was either Admiral Noyes or Captain Redmond, the director or assistant director, on the instructions of Admiral Stark.

DANFORTH: What did they say?

SAFFORD: That this was an emergency situation, we had just suffered a terrible defeat, the morale was low, that all kinds of rumors were going out from the Navy Department and we had to put a stop to this whispering campaign. It seemed perfectly logical at the time.

DANFORTH: What did you destroy yourself?

SAFFORD: I destroyed considerable notes concerning statements given to me by Lieutenant Linn and Lieutenant Commander Kramer about their handling of 14-part message, and other people who were intimately associated with them.

DANFORTH: So, there is no written record?

SAFFORD: No, sir. These were verbal reports to me. I was going to make up a consolidated report which every one would sign when we had all the facts straightened out.

DANFORTH: Just what did he say, as near as you can recall it? Give me your best recollection, that is all I want, Captain.

SAFFORD: He said, "If you have any notes or anything in writing, destroy them because somebody might see them and start something which you don't intend." It seemed a perfectly logical and fair order at the time.

DANFORTH: You had no idea, did you, Captain, that you were being asked to do anything that was improper or surreptitious?

SAFFORD: Absolutely not, or I would not have done it.

DANFORTH: Were you given any direction to destroy any files or official records?

SAFFORD: We were not given any instruction to destroy files or any official records.

DANFORTH: Now, did you destroy any notes as a result of that direction?

SAFFORD: I destroyed all the notes I had prepared.

DANFORTH: Did you destroy any notes that had reference to the 14-part message?

SAFFORD: Yes, I did.

DANFORTH: Thank you, Captain. I have no further questions at this time.

DANFORTH returns to desk. PROCTOR moves to podium.

PROCTOR: Captain, you stated definitely that you thought the message that came in on the 6th and 7th, known as the 14-part message, was an extremely important one as far as the breaking of our relations with Japan at that time was concerned?

SAFFORD: Yes, sir.

PROCTOR: Now, can you tell this court, in view of your statement of the importance of this 14-part message, why on the 6th of December you left at 4:30 and never took any more interest in the 14-parts message?

SAFFORD: I regarded my work as completed when that 14-part message had been intercepted, relayed to the Navy Department, broken down enough to see that we did have the correct key, and my best watch officer on duty to process it.... I figured I could do no more.

PROCTOR: And you stated that you were in your pajamas and bathrobe eating breakfast when word came of the attack on Pearl Harbor on Sunday?

SAFFORD: That is correct.

PROCTOR: Now then, you never had at any time from the time you left your office at 4:30 on Saturday, with a highly important message coming in, you never at any time inquired about that message until after the attack, did you?

SAFFORD: Not that I remember.

PROCTOR: Not that you remember. You did not call your office to find out whether the other parts had come in, or what they might say, or what the meaning might be?

SAFFORD: No, sir.

PROCTOR: No further questions.

Sits

DANFORTH: Now, when you left your office at 4:30 or thereabouts, on Saturday, were you violating any order, directive, or regulation of the Navy in so doing?

SAFFORD: On the contrary, sir. I believe the official closing hours were 1:00 o'clock, but military personnel were supposed to stay until 4:30.

DANFORTH: Now, when you were at home on Sunday, was there anything that you could have done, had you been in your office, to have accomplished more than what was done in your absence?

SAFFORD: Not one thing, sir.

DANFORTH: No further questions

COURTNEY: Captain, you are excused. You will refrain from conversing with any person whatsoever concerning the details of your testimony today.

SAFFORD: Yes, sir.

EXIT.

DANFORTH: Call Captain McCollum.

ENTER: Captain McCollum, a handsome, athletic, square-jawed man wearing aviator-type glasses. He raises his right hand.

COURTNEY: You do solemnly swear that the evidence you shall give in this court shall be the truth, the whole truth, and nothing but the truth. So help you God.

McCOLLUM: I do.

Takes the witness chair.

DANFORTH: Captain, will you please state your name, your rank and present duty for the record, please, sir?

MCCOLLUM: Arthur Howard McCollum, Captain, United States Navy. I am now assigned as commanding officer of the heavy cruiser *Helena.*

DANFORTH: Captain, where were you born?

MCCOLLUM: I was born in Nagasaki, Japan.

DANFORTH: And how long have you been in the Navy?

MCCOLLUM: I have been in the Navy for 28 years continuously.

DANFORTH: During the months of October and November 1941 what was your assignment?

MCCOLLUM: I was head of the Far Eastern section of the Division of Naval Intelligence.

DANFORTH: Now, as part of your duties as chief of the Far Eastern section, was it part of your duties to keep track of the Japanese fleet movements?

MCCOLLUM: It was.

DANFORTH: Did the time come in November 1941 when you determined that the Intelligence Office in Washington had lost track of part of the Japanese fleet?

MCCOLLUM: By the time you speak of, we were almost wholly dependent on one form of radio intelligence for information concerning the Japanese fleet. That form is known as traffic analysis, whereby inferences are drawn from such things as the volume of radio traffic and call signs and so on.

After a fleet has been in port a certain length of time, in the absence of other information a doubt arises as to whether those ships are where radio intelligence thinks that they are. That situation existed, to my mind, from the middle of November on.

DANFORTH: And as a result of that doubt, did you cause to be prepared on or about December 1, 1941, a memorandum showing the disposition or location of the Japanese fleet?

MCCOLLUM: Yes, sir.

DANFORTH: And was that communicated to the Commander-in-Chief of the Pacific Fleet?

MCCOLLUM: So far as I know, it was not, sir.

DANFORTH: Why not?

MCCOLLUM: I took it to my chief, Admiral Wilkinson, early Monday morning. He read this document over, directed me to wait in his office and disappeared. He came back in about 10 minutes and said: *"You be ready to go to the office of Admiral Stark with me between 11:00 and 11:30 this morning, and make a number of copies of this thing that you have given me."*

Present in that meeting were Admiral Stark, Admiral Ingersoll, Admiral Turner, of course my chief, Admiral Wilkinson, and one or two other flag officers—I believe Admirals Brainard and Noyes.

Copies of this memorandum were passed to each of the flag officers present. I then read the memorandum personally...and pointed out that in my opinion war or rupture of diplomatic relations was imminent, and I requested information as to whether or not the fleets in the Pacific had been adequately alerted.

I was given a categorical assurance by Admiral Turner that dispatches fully alerting the fleets and placing them on a war basis had already been sent. However, I had seen no such dispatches at that time.

DANFORTH: Captain, did there come a time when you prepared another dispatch to go to the various outposts. Did you prepare any such dispatch?

MCCOLLUM: About the middle of the week of 1 to 7 December I drafted a dispatch...outlining the information from the December 1 memorandum, but greatly condensed. I went further and stated we felt everything pointed to an imminent outbreak of hostilities between Japan and the United States.

That dispatch was taken by me and Captain Heard...to see Admiral Wilkinson. I was directed to take that dispatch and present it for the consideration of Admiral Turner, the Director of the War Plans Division.

Admiral turner read the dispatch over. He then made a number of changes in it, striking out all except the information parts of it. He then showed me for the first time the dispatch which he had sent on the 27th.

I said I did not think his message was enough. I said, "I would like to see mine go too." Turner said, "Well if you want to send it, you either send it the way I corrected it, or take it back to Wilkinson and we will argue about it!"—or words to that effect.

I took it back to Admiral Wilkinson and discussed it with him; and he said, "Leave it here with me for a while," and that is the last I heard of it.

COURTNEY turns to address McCollum.

COURTNEY: The Court wishes to inquire of the witness. This purported message drawn by you is not in evidence, and is not in existence?

MCCOLLUM: As I explained, sir, this sort of thing was merely my recommendation on a dispatch blank, drafted in dispatch form.

COURTNEY: But it is not in existence?

MCCOLLUM: No, sir, it is not in existence. I might explain. When the dispatch does not go out, you wad it up and throw it in the wastebasket. That is probably what happened in this case.

COURTNEY: Thank you. *(To DANFORTH)* You may resume.

DANFORTH: Captain McCollum, do you recall the date that this took place?

MCCOLLUM: It was either the 4th or 5th of December, sir, Thursday or Friday.

DANFORTH: I just wanted the members of the court to be aware of what day these dates fall on.

Flips notepad to next page

DANFORTH: Captain, do you know whether that contemplated message was ever taken to Admiral Stark?

MCCOLLUM: No, sir; I do not.

DANFORTH: Whether he passed on it, or not?

MCCOLLUM: No, sir; I do not know that.

DANFORTH walks over to desk, picks up piece of paper.

DANFORTH: Captain, what type of messages were decrypted at Pearl Harbor, if you know?

MCCOLLUM: Until about 1941, we had only, it is my understanding, a very rudimentary organization in Honolulu. At that time we were very fortunate in having become available the services of Captain Rochefort, who is the only officer in our Navy who is a top-flight cryptographer and radio man, and who also has a thorough knowledge of the Japanese language.

Rochefort was in the process of building up that organization with the primary job of making an effort to break Japanese naval codes and ciphers when the war started. He did not get very much help, I believe, from Washington.

DANFORTH: Do you know whether Admiral Turner thought that the organization in Hawaii had the capability to decode Japanese diplomatic codes?

MCCOLLUM: This is hearsay, Mr. Counselor, but I have recently heard him say he thought so, sir.

DANFORTH: Now we will go to...what's known as the "14-part message," part of which arrived on Saturday, December 6. Were you on duty at that time?

MCCOLLUM: Yes, sir.

DANFORTH: When did you receive the first 13 parts of that message?

MCCOLLUM: I was receiving parts of that message

as they came in. I was down in my office until late Saturday night, sir.

DANFORTH: Did you stay on duty until that entire message had been received?

MCCOLLUM: About 9 o'clock I went home to get some sleep so I could be bright-eyed the next morning, sir. They called me at my home in the middle of the night and told me the rest of it had come in, but they did not have the last part, there was still one to come.

DANFORTH: What time did the 14th part of that message come in on Sunday morning?

MCCOLLUM: I received it, I think, about 9 o'clock, sir. I came on duty Sunday morning prior to 8 o'clock, probably about 7:45. I do not remember the times precisely.

DANFORTH: Was Admiral Stark there when this message was brought to your office?

MCCOLLUM: The sequence of events on Sunday morning was something like this, if you are interested—

DANFORTH: I know the Court is very much interested in this particular phase of it.

MCCOLLUM: I was trying to digest the 13 parts of this thing when I received word that Admiral

Wilkinson, my chief, desired to see me. I went up to Admiral Wilkinson's office and we discussed the first 13 parts of this dispatch. I would say around 9 o'clock or a little later, an orderly came in and said Admiral Stark had come into his office, and Admiral Wilkinson said, "Well, come on, let's go and see the chief."

About a half-hour later—I was still in Admiral Stark's office—when word was sent that one of my officers wished to see me, and I stepped out, and Commander Kramer was standing there with the "delivery" part of the message; that is, an additional dispatch which directed the Japanese Ambassadors in Washington to deliver this note at 1 o'clock Washington time.

DANFORTH: What time would you say it was that you and Admiral Stark discussed it?

MCCOLLUM: Certainly before 10 o'clock, sir. At that time the suggestion was made that an additional warning be sent to Pearl Harbor.

DANFORTH: By whom?

MCCOLLUM: Admiral Wilkinson, sir. Some little discussion went on, and, as far as I know, nothing was done at that time.

DANFORTH: Was there a significance to 1 o'clock?

MCCOLLUM: Kramer had converted that time to West Coast time, Honolulu time, Manila time, and

Tokyo time, and written down on a piece of paper and shown to Admiral Stark. The suggestion was made at that time that this indicated that if anything was going to occur, it would probably start about that time.

DANFORTH: What was Admiral Stark's response?

MCCOLLUM: As I remember it, Admiral Stark picked up the telephone and attempted to contact someone over the telephone. It was my impression at the time that he tried to get General Marshall, the Chief of Staff of the Army, and had been unsuccessful in getting through.

DANFORTH: Did anything else occur?

MCCOLLUM: By this time a good many of the senior officers had come in. Admiral Turner was there, Admiral Ingersoll was there, Admiral Brainard, Admiral Noyes, and of course, my chief, Admiral Wilkinson.

Later on, about 11 o'clock, I was given to understand that it had been decided to send a warning to the forces in Hawaii, including the fleet, and that warning dispatch would be handled by the Chief of Staff of the Army.

DANFORTH: Coming back to the meeting at Admiral Stark's office on Sunday morning after you had the 1 o'clock delivery date for the message, did any officer at that meeting suggest Pearl Harbor was a possible point of attack?

MCCOLLUM: Pearl Harbor as such was never mentioned.

DANFORTH: Never mentioned?

MCCOLLUM: No, sir.

DANFORTH: Now, do I understand that the Navy did not consider this any more important than to send it to the Army and then have the Army look up the Commander-in-Chief in the Pacific and give him a copy of it? Is that how you treated it?

MCCOLLUM: That was not my decision, sir.

DANFORTH: Whose decision was that?

MCCOLLUM: That decision was made by the Chief of Naval Operations.

DANFORTH: And you talked with Admiral Stark and showed him the significance of the "delivery message" being 7:30 at Pearl Harbor?

MCCOLLUM: Yes, sir.

DANFORTH: And it was your estimate that a message should go to the admiral of the fleet no matter where it was?

MCCOLLUM: That is correct, sir.

DANFORTH: And to go immediately because you

expected something to happen at 1 o'clock, Washington time?

MCCOLLUM: That is correct, sir.

DANFORTH: Well, at any rate you have direct knowledge of the facts as to what occurred there because you were present?

MCCOLLUM: I was there.

DANFORTH: Now what did you say the significance was?

MCCOLLUM: I felt that if the Japanese intended to have war with us, they would strike at or near 1 o'clock Washington time, sir.

DANFORTH: You felt they would commence hostilities against us at 1 o'clock?

MCCOLLUM: That is correct, sir.

DANFORTH: Thank you, Captain. *(Turns to PROCTOR.)* You may examine.

PROCTOR rises and walks to podium. DANFORTH sits. Kimmel passes note to DANFORTH.

PROCTOR: Now, am I correct in assuming that you had not had previous knowledge of the contents of the message sent to Admiral Kimmel on the 27th of November?

MCCOLLUM: I had no knowledge of that other than the statement made to me on the 1st by both Admiral Stark and Admiral Turner, that the fleet had received adequate and categorical warning, sir.

PROCTOR: Now, on the day that you discussed the message that you proposed sending, did you see the message, the so-called war-warning message?

MCCOLLUM: The message was then shown to me by Admiral Turner, sir.

PROCTOR: Is that the first time you had actually seen the contents of that message?

MCCOLLUM: Yes, sir.

PROCTOR: Now, when you saw for the first time when it was shown to you by Admiral Turner, containing the words, "This is a war warning," would that have been sufficient notice to you, as an officer of the fleet, to put you on notice that war was about to break out?

MCCOLLUM: That would have been my reaction, sir.

PROCTOR: Now, if you read the entire message, was there anything in that message that would lead you, that day, as an experienced naval officer, to assume that war was going to break out at Pearl Harbor?

MCCOLLUM: I think that a commander to whom such a message is addressed must assume that war is going to break out.

PROCTOR: Thank you, Captain. That is all.

Returns to desk. DANFORTH rises

DANFORTH: Well, if you wanted to alert Admiral Kimmel to an imminent air attack on Hawaii, there would be very simple words you could do that in, wouldn't there?

MCCOLLUM: Probably so.

DANFORTH: It was your duty, was it not, to help draw up these alerts?

MCCOLLUM: No, sir.

DANFORTH: That was not your duty?

MCCOLLUM: No, sir. That duty was taken away from me in about February 1941, sir.

DANFORTH: In February of 1941 that duty was taken away from you?

MCCOLLUM: That is correct, sir.

DANFORTH: And placed where?

MCCOLLUM: Placed with Admiral Turner in the War Plans Division.

DANFORTH: That is all.

COURTNEY looks toward PROCTOR, who shakes head.

COURTNEY: You are excused You will refrain from conversing with anyone outside this courtroom concerning your testimony today.

MCCOLLUM: Yes, sir.

EXIT

DANFORTH: I would like to call Admiral Rochefort.

ENTER Captain Rochefort, slope-shouldered, jug-eared, pasty-faced man with sunken eyes and a bemused expression.

COURTNEY: You do solemnly swear that the evidence you shall give in this court shall be the truth, the whole truth, and nothing but the truth. So help you God.

ROCHEFORT: I do.

Takes the witness chair.

COURTNEY: What is your rank?

ROCHEFORT: I was about to thank the Court for promoting me. I am actually a captain.

Laughter

COURTNEY: You are not averse to a real promotion if it comes your way, I suppose.

ROCHEFORT: I would appreciate it sir.

Laughter

DANFORTH: Captain, will you state your name, rank, and present station?

ROCHEFORT: Joseph John Rochefort, Captain. I am officer in charge of the Combat Intelligence Unit at Pearl Harbor.

DANFORTH: When did you assume these duties?

ROCHEFORT: In June, 1941.

DANFORTH: What were your duties during November and December 1941?

ROCHEFORT: Very briefly, sir, to find out about all the Japanese cryptographic systems.

DANFORTH: What experience had you had in connection with cryptographic work?

ROCHEFORT: During the period 1925 to 1927, I was in charge of all cryptographic work in the Navy Department in Washington. I had, subsequently, three years in Japan as a language officer, and on various staffs had carried out cryptographic research.

DANFORTH: Do you speak Japanese?

ROCHEFORT: Yes, sir.

DANFORTH: Proceed, and give us a little detail as to the scope of your duties with your assignment in Hawaii.

ROCHEFORT: The primary duty consisted of intercepting all Japanese naval traffic, and attacking all the Japanese naval systems contained in that traffic with the exception of one system, which was being worked on in Washington, and in Corregidor.

DANFORTH: How many Japanese codes and ciphers were in use by Japan during November and December that it was your duty to intercept?

ROCHEFORT: Of the regular systems...approximately eight to ten.

DANFORTH: Now, were there any Japanese naval codes that you could intercept, but not allowed to translate, at Hawaii.

ROCHEFORT: Yes, sir.

DANFORTH: Were you able to handle by deciphering what is known as the "purple" code?

ROCHEFORT: No, sir. That was a diplomatic system.

DANFORTH: Give me the designations of the other codes you could not handle.

ROCHEFORT: J-19.

DANFORTH: That was a naval system?

ROCHEFORT: Yes, sir.

DANFORTH: Were the limitations on your duties to handle and decode the result of a working relationship between you and Washington?

ROCHEFORT: Yes, sir.

DANFORTH: Then it is very definite, is it not, that there never was any time prior to the attack on Pearl Harbor when your station in Hawaii was allowed to handle any of the "purple" or other high Japanese code transmissions?

ROCHEFORT: No sir; we were not allowed handle them.

DANFORTH: The fact is, Captain, that your activities there were definitely confined to Japanese ship movements, and other matters connected with naval operations which came in codes which you were allowed to handle and translate?

ROCHEFORT: Yes, sir.

DANFORTH: And did not include diplomatic intercepts, which, it was your understanding, were being handled by Washington, and at Corregidor?

ROCHEFORT: Yes, sir.

DANFORTH: No further questions.

DANFORTH returns to desk. PROCTOR moves to podium.

PROCTOR: Captain Rochefort, as I understand it, each day at Pearl Harbor you prepared an intelligence summary, which would be presented to Admiral Kimmel?

ROCHEFORT: Yes, sir.

PROCTOR: It is a fact, is it not, that in your daily intelligence summaries, you stated definitely and positively that the Japanese appeared to be preparing for a major offensive in the Pacific?

ROCHEFORT: Yes, sir.

PROCTOR: Now then, the fact is you did, on your daily intelligence summary, show that the Japanese aircraft carriers were not accounted for, did you not?

ROCHEFORT: As I recall, we said, "Nothing is known about the carriers."

PROCTOR: Now, the fact is that you did say in your summaries that they could not be accounted for, and then you gave that to Captain Layton, and Captain Layton went to Admiral Kimmel, and presented it to him, and Admiral Kimmel said to Captain Layton, "You mean to say they might even be coming around Diamond Head?" Do you remember that?

ROCHEFORT: I had heard that later, sir.

DANFORTH: (Rises in his seat.) Move to strike, if the Court please. It is clearly hearsay.

COURTNEY: Sustained.

PROCTOR: No further questions.

PROCTOR returns to desk. DANFORTH goes to podium and begins redirect

DANFORTH: Captain Rochefort, what was the connection of your unit with other U.S. naval units of a similar character?

ROCHEFORT: The main unit, being in Washington, controlled the duties of the other two field units. We were specifically told to keep away or not to exploit the so-called five-number systems. That was being done elsewhere.

DANFORTH: Was the J-19 a so-called five-number system?

ROCHEFORT: Yes sir. In other words, the reason we did not have these messages, the reason we did not intercept them, the reason we did not work on them or read them, was because it was not our assignment but was being handled by Washington.

DANFORTH: Did there come a time when you were allowed to work on the five-number system?

ROCHEFORT: Yes, sir. When Admiral Nimitz took over command of the Pacific Fleet, he immediately authorized us to begin work on breaking the five-number code, saying that he needed all the information on enemy ship movements that he could get.

DANFORTH: Did you have any success in breaking the five-number code?

PROCTOR *(Stands at desk.)* Objection, if the court please. Relevance

COURTNEY: Overruled. I'll allow it.

PROCTOR sits down.

ROCHEFORT: By 18 January, we had deciphered enough fragments of the JN-25 code that allowed us to estimate enemy task forces moving toward Truk and New Guinea; and by March 18,1942 we were able to read the code in real time. Information gathered on Japanese ship movements from this code was instrumental in allowing us to intercept and destroy the Japanese Fleet at Midway.

DANFORTH: And you have been recommended for the Distinguished Service Medal for that feat?

ROCHEFORT: Yes, sir.

DANFORTH: Captain, Captain Safford has testified that your code-breaking unit in Hawaii was the best skilled and most experienced code-breaking unit we had; and Captain McCollum testified that you were the Navy's only top-flight cryptographer who was also a Japanese language expert. Let me put this question to you: With your success in breaking the JN-25 code, is there any reason to believe that if Washington had not prohibited you from working on the five-number code in the months preceding Pearl Harbor, you might have successfully estimated the Japanese fleet movements toward Pearl Harbor?

ROCHEFORT: Well, I—

PROCTOR: (*Jumps to his feet.*) Objection. Clearly irrelevant.

COURTNEY: Overruled. You may answer.

ROCHEFORT: I would like to think so.

DANFORTH: *(Smiles impishly.)* No further questions

Sits

COURTNEY: You are excused. You will refrain from conversing with anyone outside this courtroom concerning the testimony you have given today.

ROCHEFORT: Yes, sir.

EXIT

COURTNEY: This looks like a good spot to take a 10-minute recess.

Stage Lights Darken. House lights go up.

* * *

ACT III: The Verdict

ORDERLY: All rise!

COURTNEY: Court is in session. Be seated, please.

All sit.

COURTNEY: Call your next witness.

DANFORTH: Call Admiral William Pye

ENTER Admiral Pye, a forceful and self-confident officer. He raises his right hand.

COURTNEY: You do solemnly swear that the evidence you shall give in this court shall be the truth, the whole truth, and nothing but the truth. So help you God.

PYE: I do.

Takes the witness chair.

DANFORTH: State your name, rank, and present station.

PYE: Vice Admiral William S. Pye, U.S. Navy, at present on active duty in the Naval War College.

DANFORTH: Will you state what duties you were performing in the year 1941?

PYE: In January 1941, I became Commander Battle Force, U.S. Pacific Fleet.

DANFORTH: Where were you at 0755 on the morning of December 7, 1941?

PYE: I was at the Halekulani Hotel in Honolulu.

DANFORTH: The task force which you commanded was in port at that time, Admiral?

PYE: It was.

DANFORTH: How long previous to the morning of 7 December 1941 had the task force which you commanded, and you yourself, along with it, been in Pearl Harbor—how many days?

PYE: We reported on Thursday, approximately the 27th of November 1941.

DANFORTH: Who was the Senior Officer Embarked in Pearl Harbor during the period of time that you and your Task Force were in Pearl Harbor?

PYE: I was.

DANFORTH: Did you, as Senior Officer Embarked in Pearl Harbor, set the condition of readiness for ships in the United States Pacific Fleet at Pearl Harbor when you were in port?

PYE: The condition of readiness was in excess of that required by condition 3. What was in effect was the result of an order previously issued by the Commander-in-Chief Pacific Fleet, directing that antiaircraft guns of all ships be available for immediate action. Each battleship had two 5-inch antiaircraft guns in readiness, and two machine guns manned, in addition to the antiaircraft control.

DANFORTH: Was it necessary for these crews to be awake and alert while they were on watch?

PYE: They were required to be on deck in the vicinity of the guns, communications manned with the antiaircraft control. I should like to add to that that the condition in which the Fleet was based at that time, being inside of the defended port, it was assumed that we would have at least from three to five minutes notice of any possible air raid attack. To have maintained people immediately at the guns during all this long period would have resulted in tiring them out and without beneficial results in case of an attack. We had every reason to suppose that the crews on deck would be able to man their guns after information was received of a possible approach of an enemy.

DANFORTH: If a ship, under the conditions of security that you maintained at Pearl Harbor between 27 November and 7 December, 1941, had gone to General Quarters at any time day or night, would the officers and men that were required to remain on board be sufficient in number and adequately trained to man all your antiaircraft guns?

PYE: Yes, they would have been. The organization of each section was such that all antiaircraft guns and directors could be manned and the personnel had been trained, using the engineers group when necessary to complete the crews.

DANFORTH: Were any of the ships present in Pearl Harbor at the time of the Japanese attack on the morning of 7 December equipped with Radar?

PYE: Yes, the *Pennsylvania* and the *California*.

DANFORTH: Preceding the attack on Pearl Harbor, that is, preceding 0755 on the morning of 7 December 1941, were any of the ships' radars being manned?

PYE: No. Ship radars in port could not be used effectively because of the interference of hills and the buildings at the Navy Yard.

DANFORTH hands PYE a document

DANFORTH: I show you EXHIBIT 4, which is the Chief of Naval Operations' dispatch of 24 November 1941, which sets out briefly that the chances of favorable negotiations with Japan are very doubtful; an aggressive movement in any direction is indicated, including possible attack on the Philippines or Guam. Had you seen this dispatch prior to 7 December 1941?

PYE: Yes.

DANFORTH: How did you interpret this dispatch?

PYE: In my opinion this dispatch is subject to several interpretations. In the first place, it mentions an aggressive movement in any direction, including attack on the Philippines or Guam as a possibility. It therefore did not indicate that the aggressive action was to be necessarily against the United States. The only significant part of this message, in my opinion, is including the possibility that the enemy might take the initiative by attacking the Philippines or Guam. The fact that the Philippines and Guam are mentioned indicate that it is the estimate of the author of the dispatch and probably places a limitation, in his mind, as to the extent of the aggressive movement against the United States.

DANFORTH hands PYE a document.

DANFORTH: I show you EXHIBIT 5, which is a Chief of Naval Operations' dispatch of 27 November 1941. It contains the information that the dispatch is a war warning, that an aggressive move by Japan is expected within the next few days, and directs the execution of an appropriate defensive deployment preparatory to carrying out the tasks assigned in WPL-46. Do you recall when you first saw or were informed of the contents of this dispatch?

PYE: I saw the dispatch on Saturday, the 29th of November.

DANFORTH: Do you recall any decisions that were made based on the information you had current with this dispatch?

PYE: This dispatch was discussed at some length with the Commander-in-Chief. The significance of the first clause, "This dispatch is to be considered a war warning," was, in my mind, nothing more than we had been receiving at various times during the past year. We had known since September 1939 that there was a possibility of war, and every endeavor was being made by those in the Fleet to carry out its plans.

It is significant, I think, to note that this dispatch is a multiple address dispatch. It is addressed, first, to the Commander-in-Chief Asiatic

Fleet and second, to the Commander-in-Chief Pacific Fleet. As far as any strategic deployment of the Pacific Fleet was concerned, the execution of WPL-46 required the Fleet to depart from Pearl Harbor. There were no other elements of the strategic deployment that were available at this particular time other than to proceed toward the West Coast. There were at this time no carriers in port.

A Fleet at sea without carriers, sighted by a force of such characters as to have a chance of a successful attack on the Hawaiian Islands, would be more subject to defeat than a force in port guarded by presumably several hundred fighting planes of the Army at the base. We did not believe that under the circumstances it was necessary to take any further action. To take the Fleet to sea would likely have subjected it to possible enemy submarine attack, from which it was guarded in port.

DANFORTH: How about an air attack, along the same line?

PYE: I have stated that the Fleet at sea would have been in greater danger from air attack than they would have been in port guarded by several hundred fighter planes.

DANFORTH: In your opinion, what was the condition of the state of training of personnel of your force and in the Fleet, that is, the Pacific Fleet, at the time of the attack on Pearl Harbor?

PYE: After over four years continuously in the Fleet up to then, I considered the state of training the highest I had ever seen since I had been in the Fleet.

DANFORTH: Well, considering the possibility of any form of attack on Pearl Harbor, do you feel that everything possible had been done in the Fleet to meet an attack, so far as your vessels, personnel, planes, and other control conditions available were concerned?

PYE: Before the event, it was my opinion that the defense measures taken were consistent with the situation.

DANFORTH: Thank you, Admiral.

DANFORTH turns and starts back to desk as if finished, then suddenly turns back toward witness.

DANFORTH: Oh, yes, Admiral, one more question. What is your assessment of Admiral Kimmel's performance as Commander-in-Chief, Pacific Fleet?

PYE: I would like to state as my definite opinion that Admiral Kimmel was a most efficient Commander-in-Chief. I firmly believed that he was as good as any other officer that could have been selected. He had shown a tremendous interest in the tactical development of the Fleet while in the Command of Cruisers, and he and I had worked continuously together for six months trying to develop the tactics of light forces. In this respect, his interest was superior to those of any Commander-in-Chief I had served with. He was also tremendously interested in the material and logistic support of the Fleet, and worked conscientiously in all respects to bring the Fleet to its highest state of readiness in preparation for war.

DANFORTH: And is that still your opinion?

PYE: Yes, it is.

DANFORTH: No further questions.

COURTNEY looks toward PROCTOR, who shakes his head.

COURTNEY: Admiral, you are excused. You will not discuss with anyone outside this courtroom concerning your testimony today.

PYE: Yes, sir.

EXIT

DANFORTH: Call Admiral Claude Bloch

ENTER Admiral Bloch, a round-faced, nearly bald man. He raises right hand.

COURTNEY: You do solemnly swear that the evidence you shall give in this court shall be the truth, the whole truth, and nothing but the truth. So help you God.

BLOCH: I do.

Takes the witness chair.

DANFORTH: State your name, rank, and present station.

BLOCH: Claude D. Bloch, Admiral, U.S. Navy, retired, on active duty as a member of the General Board.

DANFORTH: What duties were you performing during the year 1941?

BLOCH: Commandant 14th Naval District.

DANFORTH: Were you performing any duties in conjunction with the Army?

BLOCH: Yes.

DANFORTH: What were they, in brief?

BLOCH: I was performing duties prescribed by the Navy Regulations and directives from the Commander-in-Chief, Pacific Fleet.

DANFORTH: Will you state what the Army task was, according to section 3 of JCD-42?

BLOCH: The Army task was to hold Oahu against attack by sea, land, and air forces, and against hostile sympathizers; to support the naval forces.

DANFORTH: What is the Navy task?

BLOCH: The Navy task—to patrol the coastal zones and to control and protect shipping lanes; to support Army forces.

DANFORTH: Do you recall what condition of readiness was in effect in the 14th Naval District on the night of 6 December 1941?

BLOCH: There was a fleet order to maintain readiness Condition 3. The ships in the harbor had their guns ready and ammunition at the guns, and a large percentage of officers and men on board.

DANFORTH approaches witness chair and hands a document to Bloch.

DANFORTH: I show you EXHIBIT 20, which is the Chief of Naval Operations dispatch of 28 November, 1941, and refers to a message sent by the Army to Commander Western Defense Command. Please inspect the subject matter contained in this dispatch and inform the Court whether you were familiar with its contents around the time of its probable receipt in Hawaii?

BLOCH: I saw the dispatch. The items in the dispatch that made the biggest impression on me were that part concerning the desire of the United States to have Japan make the first hostile act, and the other part was concerning not to alarm the public. By implication, it was my belief that it was obligatory upon the Navy to consider these same restrictions.

DANFORTH: Who did you, Admiral, consider was responsible for the defense of Pearl Harbor?

BLOCH: The Army, absolutely.

DANFORTH: Do you recall if you had any conference with the Commander-in-Chief of the Pacific Fleet before December 7, 1941, with reference to the information contained in this dispatch?

BLOCH: Yes, I think so.

DANFORTH: During this conference, did you express your ideas to the Commander-in-Chief and to other officers present as to what kind of attack, if any, which could be expected?

BLOCH: Expected where, sir?

DANFORTH: Expected at Pearl Harbor?

BLOCH: The only information which I had was contained in the dispatch of November 27, in which there is nothing said indicating an attack on Pearl Harbor.

DANFORTH: But, Admiral, in discussing this dispatch was there any kind of discussion as to what kind of attack that might come from Japan?

BLOCH: I believe there was full and free discussion by all members who were present, and that, without exception, everyone believed the dispatch indicated an attack on Southeast Asia.

DANFORTH: Thank you, Admiral. No further questions

DANFORTH returns to his desk. PROCTOR half rises.

PROCTOR: No questions, your Honor.

COURTNEY: You are excused. You will not discuss with anyone outside this courtroom concerning your testimony today.

BLOCH: Yes, sir.

EXIT

DANFORTH: Call Lieutenant Colonel Tyler

ENTER: Lt. Col Tyler, a boyish-looking man of about 30, in Air Corps uniform with wings and campaign ribbons. He raises his right hand.

COURTNEY: You do solemnly swear that the evidence

you shall give in this court shall be the truth, the whole truth, and nothing but the truth. So help you God.

TYLER: I do.

Takes the witness chair.

DANFORTH: Will you state your name, rank, and present station?

TYLER: Kermit A. Tyler, Lieutenant Colonel, Air Corps, Army Air Force Board, Orlando, Florida.

DANFORTH: What was your rank and duty on 7 December 1941?

TYLER: I was assigned as Executive Officer in the 8th Pursuit Squadron. I was a first lieutenant at that time.

DANFORTH: What duties were you performing at about 0755 on the morning of 7 December 1941?

TYLER: I was assigned duty as Assistant to the Controller, at the information center at Fort Shafter, Hawaii.

DANFORTH: Will you tell the Court in a brief way what these duties consisted of?

TYLER: The duty was to assist the Controller in ordering planes to intercept enemy planes, or supposed enemy planes. I was sent down there for training.

DANFORTH: Were you in a branch of an information center, or at an information center, or what?

TYLER: At the one information center for all of the islands.

DANFORTH: At the one information center for all of the islands. Now, were you in contact with all of the radar stations?

TYLER: Yes, sir, they all had direct lines.

DANFORTH: Now, were you the Senior Officer Present at this central station or post?

TYLER: I was the only officer present.

DANFORTH: Now, did you receive, while you were on duty on the morning of the 7th of December 1941, any report of interest?

TYLER: How do you mean by that, sir?

DANFORTH: Did you receive any information or any report that you considered of any importance?

TYLER: Well, I received a call from one of the radar stations, I believe it is called Opana, which indicated that they had a large number of planes that he had not seen before on his scope.

DANFORTH: Can you recall at about what time this report was received at the station?

TYLER: I would estimate it was around 7:15.

DANFORTH: Now where is this Opana station located from where you say you got this report?

TYLER: It was on the north side of the island.

DANFORTH: Can you remember the language of the report?

TYLER: I can't remember the exact language. As I said before, the radar operator reported that he had a larger plot than he had previously seen. That is about all there is to it.

DANFORTH: Now exactly, again, Colonel, what information did this radar operator give you when he made the report?

TYLER: He said that at a distance of around 130 miles, he had a larger plot that he had ever seen on his scope.

DANFORTH: Did you have any abnormal reaction to this report at that time?

TYLER: No, sir. I thought about it for a minute, and then told him, "Thanks for calling in the report."

DANFORTH: No effort was made to pass this information along that you first got about 7:15 in the morning?

TYLER: No, sir; that is right.

DANFORTH: Well, did it occur to you at all that it might be an attack and that it should be passed along?

TYLER: No, sir; it did not.

DANFORTH: Well, did you make any effort from any source to find out whether this flight was foreign, or local?

TYLER: No, sir.

DANFORTH: No further questions.

PROCTOR: I do not desire to queston this witness.

COURTNEY: You are excused. You will not discuss with anyone outside this courtroom concerning your testimony today.

EXIT

DANFORTH: Call Admiral Halsey.

ENTER Admiral Halsey, a tall, gaunt, gruff, forceful man with bushy eyebrows and furrowed brow. All eyes look on this legendary figure with awe as he walks toward the witness chair.

COURTNEY: You do solemnly swear that the evidence you shall give in this court shall be the truth, the whole truth, and nothing but the truth. So help you God.

HALSEY: I do.

Takes the witness chair.

DANFORTH: Admiral, please state your name, rank, and present station.

HALSEY: William F. Halsey, Admiral, U.S. Navy, Commanding South Pacific Area and Third Fleet.

DANFORTH: Sir, you have a long and illustrious naval career, on which we all congratulate you.

HALSEY: Thank you.

DANFORTH: Sir, what duties were you performing on 7 December 1941?

HALSEY: I was Commander Aircraft Battle Force and Commander Task Force Two at Pearl Harbor. I assumed that command in June 1940.

DANFORTH: Sir, how much of October and November 1941 were you at sea?

HALSEY: Approximately two-thirds of the time.

DANFORTH: Sir, on what date did you leave Pearl Harbor prior to December 7?

HALSEY: The last date I left prior to December 7 was the 28th of November. When I left with my task force that morning, I did not let anyone know where we were going until we were clear of the harbor. At that point I peeled off the battleships and destroyers that were not to accompany us. I went off to the westward, and sent them off to the southward and eastward where they returned to port.

DANFORTH: During the latter half of 1941, what did you consider the primary mission of the Pacific Fleet?

HALSEY: To prepare for war with Japan.

DANFORTH: Do you feel that Admiral Kimmel was of like opinion, that he considered that to be the primary mission of the Fleet?

HALSEY: Absolutely.

DANFORTH: Sir, I hand you a copy of a dispatch dated 16 October 1941, which is EXHIBIT 3. Do recall the approximate time that you first saw this dispatch?

HALSEY: I believe I saw this dispatch soon after its receipt, and it caused a tremendous amount of discussion and speculation on where the Japs were likely to strike. Because Guam and the Philippines were specifically mentioned in the dispatch, we thought more along those lines than of a surprise attack on Hawaii.

DANFORTH: Sir, I hand you what has been admitted as Exhibit 5, a dispatch dated November 27, 1941. Do you recall seeing this dispatch?

HALSEY: I probably saw this dispatch at the conference that took place on the morning of the 27th of November. I was with Admiral Kimmel from nine a.m. to around six p.m. that day. I believe there were preliminary dispatches before that conference, and that it came to a head that day. The decision was made to send fighter planes to Wake Island. Their field was just then ready for use.

Admiral Stark had suggested sending fighter planes to Wake and Midway. It was decided to send Navy and Marine planes because the Army was not allowed to fly their planes farther than 15 miles from the coast, partly because their pilots had little experience flying over water. The next day I sailed for Wake with 12 planes on the *Enterprise*, and Admiral Brown sailed for Midway with 12 planes on the *Lexington*.

DANFORTH: On that day, were you concerned for the security of Pearl Harbor?

HALSEY: No, sir.

DANFORTH: Sir, at that time, what was your interpretation of the wording "preparatory deployment" in this dispatch?

HALSEY: I believe that it was decided that the task forces at sea and in port were acting in a preparatory deployment, ready to go in case the order was given. Submarines were sent to the Far East, as were B-17s. This took away a lot of our attack forces from Hawaii. Submarine patrols were established at Midway and Wake. The only planes available for Midway and Wake were sent; that is, patrol planes. This further weakened the reconnaissance from Hawaii.

DANFORTH: Sir, in general terms, would you tell us what transfers of units of the Fleet were made from the Pacific Fleet to other areas during the latter part of 1941?

HALSEY: There were three battleships, one carrier out of the four we had, and a number of cruisers and destroyers, the exact number I do not remember, but approximately 25 percent of our strength, were sent to the Atlantic. This produced a decided weakening of the Pacific Fleet and left it, according to my recollection, less strength than the Japanese Fleet.

DANFORTH: Did you feel that these transfers incapacitated the Pacific Fleet for carrying out the tasks assigned to it in the war plans?

HALSEY: I felt that it militated against our chances of success in carrying out these plans.

DANFORTH: Sir, do you know what Admiral Kimmel's reaction was to the transfer of these units of his Fleet?

HALSEY: I remember very distinctly that he was very much against the transfer; he deplored it.

DANFORTH: Sir, did you feel, at the time, that Washington kept the Pacific Fleet well informed as to what the Japs were doing?

HALSEY: I did not feel we were well informed on what the Japs were doing, and I felt we were operating in the dark. I had the personal feeling, entirely personal, that they knew a lot more in Washington than we knew out here and that we should have been informed.

DANFORTH: Do you recall any discussions that you had with Admiral Kimmel along that line, whether steps were being taken to improve the situation?

HALSEY: I recall discussions along that line and damning them for not letting us in on the information. I believe Admiral Kimmel said he would demand, or had demanded, that they give him more information.

DANFORTH: Admiral, prior to 7 December, what information did you have as to what distance aerial reconnaissance was being carried out around Oahu?

HALSEY: I was aware of the daily plan for reconnaissance. I also knew that the search planes available were limited in number, had been run very hard. It became a question, and a very serious question, and occasioned many discussions between Admiral Bellinger and Admiral Kimmel whether they should use a plane continually and keep a full coverage and have them all go to pieces at once, or put out the best partial coverage they could to keep the planes in shape so that they could be used in case of necessity. The only long-distance Army planes we had were the B-17s, and most of them had been flown out to the Philippines.

DANFORTH: Admiral, during the few days in late November, while your task force was in Pearl Harbor, do you recall any conversation or did you give any thought yourself toward a departure from the scheduled deployment by virtue of which all fleet units would have been out of Pearl Harbor?

HALSEY: I do not, and I did not.

DANFORTH: One final question, Admiral. Do you have an opinion as to Admiral Kimmel's effectiveness in preparing the Fleet for war?

HALSEY: Yes. The most vivid recollection I have is the unceasing and futile attempts of Admiral

Kimmel to secure adequate equipment and personnel. Training was the first priority. There just weren't enough airplanes to keep the carriers staffed and to establish and train replacement squadrons. I have never known a Commander-in-Chief of any United States Fleet who worked harder and under more adverse circumstances to increase its efficiency, and to prepare for war. Further, I know of no officer who might have done more than Kimmel did.

DANFORTH: Thank you Admiral. *(To PROCTOR:)* You may examine.

DANFORTH returns to desk. PROCTOR goes to podium. thumbs through his notes, seems indecisive..

PROCTOR: Admiral, are you familiar with the so-called Martin-Bellinger Report, which is marked EXHIBIT 7?

HALSEY: I am.

PROCTOR: That estimate makes specific reference to a surprise air attack on Pearl Harbor, does it not?

HALSEY: Yes, but let me say that the question of an air attack on Pearl Harbor was always at the forefront of everybody's mind. In my own personal opinion, I did not think an air attack was coming. All of the dispatches from CNO indicated that the Philippines, Guam, Borneo, and the Kra Peninsula were the most likely targets. The decisions in Washington to transfer ships to the Atlantic, fighter planes to Wake and Midway, and B-17s to Manila, and to ignore Admiral Kimmel's pleas for more equipment—all served to strengthen our opinion. Washington had the benefit of far more and better intelligence than we did. Never once did they give us the slightest indication that they had reason to believe that Pearl Harbor was the target.

PROCTER is getting nowhere and belatedly realizes the cross-examination of Admiral Halsey is only giving him more opportunity to help his old friend. Sits down.

DANFORTH: No questions.

COURTNEY: You are excused. You will not discuss with anyone outside this courtroom concerning your testimony today.

HALSEY: Yes, sir.

EXIT

DANFORTH: Call Admiral Turner.

ENTER: Admiral Turner, who takes his place in witness chair.

COURTNEY: The Court reminds you that your oath previously taken is still binding.

DANFORTH approaches the podium, documents in hand.

DANFORTH: Admiral Turner, I also desire to commend you very highly on the splendid war record that you have made. Any questions I might ask you about the period of time during which you served as Chief of War Plans of the Navy will not in any way reflect on this distinguished record you have made.

TURNER: Thank you.

DANFORTH: But I do want to inquire briefly about some matters that you have developed in your previous testimony in connection with the period of time during which you served as Chief of the War Plans Division of the Navy. And may I say that my impression is that much of the information you have given is somewhat in conflict with other information we have received during the trial. Naturally, we want to reconcile all these matters as much as we can.

TURNER: Yes, sir.

DANFORTH: Now, it was your duty and responsibility as Chief of the War Plans Division to make plans for war in case this country became involved in war?

TURNER: That is correct.

DANFORTH: And also to direct any operations that might become necessary in connection with these plans?

TURNER: To give orders for the initiation of operations and to give advice as to major changes or major aspects of the operation.

DANFORTH: Now, would it be fair to assume that from the standpoint of the real effect of operations that the War Plans Division perhaps had the highest responsibility for the advice given to the Chief of Naval Operations?

TURNER: That is correct.

DANFORTH: The Office of Naval Intelligence was largely charged with the responsibility of disseminating intelligence information?

TURNER: That is correct.

DANFORTH: But your Division, War Plans, was the responsible Operations division?

TURNER: So far as regards the major aspects of war.

DANFORTH: And you felt that owing to your broader field of operation, and the chance that your strategic estimates and those of Intelligence might conflict, you brought about an arrangement by which the Intelligence estimates on their way to the Chief of Naval Operations passed through your office, so that you could make your comment and they wouldn't be confused; is that it?

TURNER: Yes, sir.

DANFORTH: Admiral, Let me read to you pertinent parts of a memorandum from Vice Admiral Kirk to Vice Admiral Wilkinson, which is in evidence as EXHIBIT 21, and then ask you to comment on them. (Reading:)

2. On April 1941, following a discussion in the office of Admiral Ingersoll, Assistant Chief of Naval Operations, with the Director of War Plans, Rear Admiral Turner, and myself, the three of us entered the officeof Admiral Stark, Chief of Naval Operations, wherein the points at issue were reviewed.

3. It was maintained by me that the Office of Naval Intelligence was responsible for interpreting possible enemy intentions after evluating information received from whatever source. Further, that the Office of Naval Intelligence was comparable to G-2 in the War Department General Staff in these respects and should likewise prepare that section of the formal Estimate known as "Enemy Intentions."

4. This position was contested by Rear Admiral Turner who maintained that the War Plans Division should prepare such section of the Estimate, and should interpret and evaluate all information concerning possible hostile nations from whatever source received. Further, that the Office of Naval Intelligence was solely a collection agency and a distributing agency, and that it was not charged with sending out any informatiion which would initiate any operations of the fleet, or fleets,anywhere.

5. *Admiral Stark then approved the position taken by Rear Admiral Turner.*

Now, Admiral, how did you interpret this memo?

TURNER: Yes, sir. My principle point is that I did not consider this oral instruction of the Chief of Naval Operations to the Director of Naval Intelligence on this subject to be a change in existing orders, but merely an interpretation of them. It was essential that communications from the Chief of Naval Operations be consistent, and therefore that estimates which might be prepared by the Office of Naval Intelligence should be cleared through the War Plans Division.

DANFORTH: You made a statement that neither you nor Admiral Stark had any knowledge, prior to December 7, 1941, as to what, if any equipment existed at Pearl Harbor to decode or decrypt Japanese messages. Had you no information at all about that?

TURNER: On three occasions, at Admiral Stark's initiative, I asked Admiral Noyes as to whether or not Admiral Kimmel was receiving the same decrypted information that we were receiving here.

On each occasion, Admiral Noyes assured me that both Admiral Kimmel and Admiral Hart were receiving the same information that we had.

DANFORTH: Admiral Noyes would not have any reason, of course, to deceive you about such information, would he?

TURNER: Not in the least. He gave me at all times all information that I requested.

DANFORTH: Well, then, here's the situation as I see it: According to the set-up you described...it was your responsibility to keep these fleet commanders fully advised and report to them any over-all information that affected the possibilities of war; and, of course, it was not possible to discharge that duty if you did not know what means they had of obtaining information on their own. You could not do that unless you knew precisely what they already had , isn't that so?

TURNER: No, sir; that is not correct. It was not my duty to inform the commanders-in-chief as to Intelligence. It was my duty to inform them as to the major aspects of the international situation that might lead to war with the United States or might affect war with the United States.

DANFORTH: Sir, I may be confused. On the one hand, you take the position that all Intelligence to the Fleet must flow through you; and on the other hand, you say, "It was not my duty to inform the commanders-in-chief as to Intelligence." Those two things appear to be contradictory, don't they?

TURNER: Not in my mind.

DANFORTH: Admiral, at what time did you talk with Admiral Noyes about Admiral Kimmel getting "magic" and decoding it there?

TURNER: I don't remember definitely. I have a vague recollection that I first discussed it with Admiral Noyes about January 1941.

DANFORTH: How do you account then, for these letters that were put in the record the other day where Admiral Kimmel wrote to Admiral Stark on February 18, 1941:

(Reading): *"I have recently been told by an officer fresh from Washington that ONI considered it the function of War Plans to furnish the Commander-in-Chief with information of a secret nature. I have heard also that War Plans considers the responsibility for furnishing the same type of information to be that of ONI."*

Then a letter back from Stark to Kimmel on March 22: (Reading:) *"With reference to your postscript on the subject of fixing responsibility for the furnishing of secret information to CINCAF, Kirk informs me that ONI is fully aware of the responsibility for keeping you adequately informed concerning foreign nations, activities of these nations, and disloyal elements within the United States."*

How do you account for that letter if you had told Stark in January that they had the means of getting all this secret information?

TURNER: I do not believe that the word "secret" refers exclusively to magic at all.

DANFORTH: Well, now, Admiral, did you approve the message sending information that the Japanese were destroying codes? Did you send that?

TURNER: No, sir. I did not send it. I approved it.

DANFORTH: You approved it?

TURNER: Yes, sir.

DANFORTH: Why would you approve that, if you thought that they had a "purple" machine at Pearl and were getting the same messages that you were sending them? If you thought they were getting the same information, why would you send that information that came to you by virtue of magic? They would already have had it.

TURNER: That is true, but this was for the purpose of centering attention on that particular thing and I did not know—I do not believe I knew—whether that information had come—just exactly how that information had come. I had seen some dispatches, it is true, from Tokyo ordering the destruction of codes. I cannot explain to you how the mistake about—the misunderstanding—on the code occurred. It is just a mystery to me.

DANFORTH: Those two things seem to be contradictory, isn't that true?

TURNER: They seem to be, yes.

PROCTOR: (Rising:) Your Honor, I object to this line of questioning. Admiral Turner is not the person on trial here.

DANFORTH: If it please the Court, it is established fact that he who controls the flow of information often exercises great and unrecognized power. I am merely trying to get at the facts of the matter: What information did Washington pass on to Admiral Kimmel, and what information was withheld.

COURTNEY: You may continue.

DANFORTH: Well, let's pass on to something else now. There is some evidence that Captain McCollum, sometime between the first of December and the seventh of December, indicated or showed a view that some further warning ought to be sent to Pearl Harbor. Do you know anything about that?

TURNER: Yes, sir. From time to time Captain McCollum would come to me with drafts of memoranda to CNO concerning the situation and we would discuss them. I think he had such a memorandum about the first of December, but I do not believe that it was intended to go out as a dispatch but was merely for the information of the Chief of Naval Operations. Now, I have not seen such a memorandum, but I have a recollection of that.

Now, about the first or second of December—and this is sure, I am completely sure of this, I remember very distinctly—about the first or second of December, Commander McCollum came into my office and handed me a proposed dispatch written on one sheet of paper...in which he proposed that the Chief of Naval Operations send out to the fleets concerning the imminence of war. It covered the same ground approximately as the CNO dispatches of the 24th and the 27th.

Now, I know that Admiral Wilkinson and some other officers in ONI had seen these two dispatches and I asked McCollum if he had seen them.

DANFORTH: Do you mean if he had seen the officers, or seen the dispatches?

TURNER: If he had seen the two dispatches of the 24th and 27th, and he said, "No." So I pulled the two dispatches out and handed them to him and said, "Well, read these over and then see if you think your dispatch ought to go." He sat down and read them over and he said, "No," and tore up the proposed dispatch. It had the same general coverage but was not as specific as these two messages.

DANFORTH: Not as specific as those two that were sent?

TURNER: Not quite, no, sir.

DANFORTH: If Captain McCollum's message was in substantially the same language as the one you had sent on the 27th, wouldn't he be infringing on your department and wouldn't you tell him not to send it if it was in effect an operational order?

TURNER: No, sir. By no means would I have told him not to send it. As I have testified before, when the Office of Naval Intelligence wanted to send out material, even though it included strategic estimates and they cleared the matter with me and I felt it ought to go out, I would certainly approve sending it out. The decision not to send it was made entirely by Captain McCollum.

DANFORTH: Admiral, Let's go on to another matter. I understand your testimony to be that on July 26, war with Japan was certain, and that the probability of an attack on Hawaii was 50-50. Did you have that in mind at the time of the sending the dispatch of July 3, 1941?

TURNER: Yes, sir, ultimately, within the next several months.

DANFORTH: Admiral, can you point out to this Court anywhere, at any time, any single word in writing where you said that, anywhere, at any time, to anyone, where you made such a statement in writing?

TURNER: That is the 50-50?

DANFORTH: Yes. I am talking now about before December 7. Incidentally, I have never seen a poor Monday morning quarterback. What we want is what happened before December 7, 1941. Now, is there anywhere, at any time, where you said to any person anything like that in writing or to anyone in the Navy Department, any paper that will show it by anyone in the Department?

TURNER: No, not anything on the 50-50, but I invite your attention to the consideration of the Secretary of the Navy's letter of January 24 as to the strong possibilities that war would be initiated with a raid, an air raid on Hawaii.

DANFORTH: That was in the—

TURNER: On the 50-50, I was asked my opinion as to what I thought the chances were, and I said 50-50. I never put that in writing.

DANFORTH: Now, will you point out in your estimate of the situation of July 3, 1941, anything like that or indicate anything like that? That was a current estimate of the situation, wasn't it, July 3rd?

TURNER: That is not mentioned there.

DANFORTH: One final question. Sir, I note the care and speed with which the messages were delivered to the various officials in Washington, but no one thought anything was going to happen in Washington did they? It was Hawaii and the Far East that action was expected. Why was immediate knowledge of these intercepts in Washington so important, if no word of their content or significance was sent to the commander in Hawaii until too late to be of any use?

TURNER: Admiral Kimmel—

DANFORTH: *(Wheels and walks away.)* No further questions.

Sits.

PROCTOR Indicates he does not wish to question.

COURTNEY: You are excused. You will not discuss with anyone outside this courtroom concerning your testimony today.

TURNER: Yes, sir.

EXIT

COURTNEY: You may call your next witness

Kimmel rises as if to testify. DANFORTH pulls him back.

DANFORTH: If it please the Court, I request a brief recess to confer with my client.

COURTNEY: Without objection, Court will take a brief recess. Will five minutes suffice?

DANFORTH: Yes, sir.

Stage lights go our except for cone of light over Danforth and Kimmel. All members of the Court freeze in their positions, except Danforth and Kimmel who carry on an animated conversation.

DANFORTH: Admiral, I know you want to have your say. But when this case is over, you can say anything and the media will print it all. My only concern is that you win this case. So far, they have not a scintilla of evidence that you were derelict in your duties. I sincerely believe that Turner has thoroughly discredited himself. Every fact we wanted in is not only in, but is undisputed. There simply is not anything you can say that will improve this record. The case is ours to lose. Putting you on will only give a desperate prosecutor his last chance to make a case.

You know better than I that surprises, even complete surprises happen in warfare almost every day. But the public doesn't know that, and many of them think someone *has* to be at fault. So far, you have been the scapegoat. Why give them another chance to persuade the Court to their view?

KIMMEL: But what about the inference that I have something to hide?

DANFORTH: Dispel that with your post-trial press conference. Offer to answer any questions anyone might have.

Trust me on this Admiral. Don't take the stand.

Stage lights come back up. Action resumes

DANFORTH: *(Stands:)* The defense rests.

COURTNEY: The defense rests?

DANFORTH: Yes sir.

COURTNEY: Very well. Is the Judge Advocate ready with his closing argument?

PROCTOR: (Rises:) Yes, sir.

COURTNEY: You may proceed.

PROCTOR: *(Rises and goes to podium:)* May it please the Court, on December 7, 1941, the Japanese Navy was able to move a fleet of aircraft carriers and supporting ships to within 250 miles of Pearl Harbor, completely undetected. From that position they were able to launch a virtually undefended attack upon the men and ships of the Pacific Fleet anchored at Pearl Harbor.

Despite repeaed warning dispatches, the naval forces of the United States at Pearl Harbor took not one step to prepare for attack, either by aerial reconnaissance of the surrounding area or by a heightened state of alert.

No effort was made to rotate the ships of the fleet in and out of the harbor so as to keep the details of ships present from the enemy.

The fact is, if the Court please, Pearl Harbor was totally unprepared and completely surprised on that Sunday morning. This trial is about the respsonsibility for that unacceptable state of affairs. No one in this room can possibly have any doubt as to where that responsibility lies; it lies with the Commander. No armed force can function otherwise. Your duty may be unpleasant in the extreme, but it is at least clear.

Sits down.

DANFORTH: *(Rises and goes to podium.)* If the Court please, I will be brief. Closing argument in most trials is a reexamination of the evidence with a jury. No such reexamination is necessary here because this case hasn't been tried by a jury. Juries are selected for how little they know about the case; and I would be insulting the Court to suggest that my knowledge of the issues before you is greater than yours.

Suffice it to say, there is simply no evidence of dereliction of duty or any other malfeasance on the part of Admiral Kimmel. His use of the airplanes, equipment and crews available to him was entirely consistent with the consideration of maintenance and crew availability. There is no testimony that rotation of ships in and out of Pearl Harbor would have lessened Japanese intelligence on the Fleet. We are an open society. The harbor is completely open to public view. Moreover, the specification that Admiral Kimmel failed to appreciate the gravity of the situation borders on the absurd. Admiral Kimmel did not have the capacity to read Japanese dispatches by use of Purple, as did Washington and even Manila. Plus the inescapable fact is that no one, Admiral Turner not withstanding, not the Chief of Naval Operations, not the Chief of Naval intelligence, not the Chief of Staff, not even the President of the United States believed that the Japanese would make such a colossal blunder as to attack Pearl Harbor. It is not unreasonable to suspect that even Yamamoto himself had serious misgivings about the mission assigned to him.

I suggest to you that surprise attacks are frequent occurrences in battle; but to those unfamiliar with combat, there is the feeling that someone must have been at fault. I would have hoped that in making the prosecutive decision in this case, the temptation to find a scapegoat would have been resisted, but it was not.

Admiral Husband E. Kimmel, who has served our country with great skill and dedication throughout his distinguished naval career, deserves better at the hands of his countrymen. You must acquit.

Sits.

COURTNEY: Court will consider the evidence.

BLACKOUT for 30-seconds to denote passage of time. Voices are heard arguing in background.

When lights come up again, all participants are still in their places.

COURTNEY: The Court has reached a verdict. Defendant will please stand.

KIMMEL and DANFORTH stand.

COURTNEY: Admiral Husband E. Kimmel, as to the charge of dereliction of duty, it is the judgment of this Court that you be found NOT GUILTY.

KIMMEL and DANFORTH congratulate each other. Great weight seems to be lifted from KIMMEL'S shoulders.

COURTNEY: I am not finished!

KIMMEL and DANFORTH stand at attention.

COURTNEY: By directive of Admiral Ernest J. King, Chief of Naval Operations, the results of this trial, together with all testimony and proceedings, will be placed under seal and classified as Secret. No part of it may be reported to the public. Court is dismissed.

KIMMEL'S shoulders slump as lights go out.

Curtain

* * *

Epilogue

The 1944 Navy Court of Inquiry completely exonerated Admiral Kimmel of any wrongdoing. The public never learned of this fact, however, because Admiral Ernest J. King, Chief of Naval Operations, without ever having read the report, rejected the Court's findings and classified its findings and proceedings as "secret." This action prohibited the results from becoming public knowledge. A thunderstruck Admiral Kimmel was informed of this decision on the ironic date of December 7, 1944.

List of Exhibits

1. Navy Basic War Plan WPL-46
2. Stark Letter to Kimmel re Ambassador Nomura 23-Sep-1941
3. Dispatch Chief of Naval Operations to CinCPac 16-Oct-1941
4. Dispatch CNO 24-Nov-1941
5. Dispatch CNO "War Warning" 27-Nov-1941
6. SecNav Letter 24-Jan-1941
7. Martin-Bellinger Report 1-May-1941
8. Kimmel Letter to Stark 18-Feb-1941
9. Kimmel Letter to Stark 26-May-1941
10. Fitness Report of Admiral Kimmel
11. Chart of ship disposition at Pearl Harbor 7-Dec-1941
12. Battle damage report
13. Organization of the Office of Chief of Naval Operations.
14. Intelligence Division (OP-16) Duties
15. Memo CNO to Office of Naval Intelligence 12-Dec-1940
16. Stark reply to Kimmel 22-Mar-1941
17. Kirk memo to CNO 11-Mar-1941
18. Pilot - Fourteen-Part Message
19. 14th Part of Fourteen-Part Message
20. CNO dispatch re Army Western Defense Command 28-Nov-1941
21. Kirk memorandum to Wilkinson, 1945

About the Authors

James Edwin Alexander is Dean Emeritus of the Meinders School of Business at Oklahoma City University. The author or coauthor of 24 previous books, including *Prisoner of the Rising Sun*, a History Book-of-the-Month Club selection, he is listed in *Who's Who in the World* and *Who's Who in Finance and Industry*. Alexander is retired from the Naval Reserve with the rank of Chief Warrant Officer. He holds a doctorate from Vanderbilt University.

William R. Burkett is a former District Judge, U.S. Attorney, State Representative, and Presiding Judge of the Oklahoma Temporary Court of Appeals. He is coauthor (with Alexander) of *The Fall of David Hall*. As an Army Lieutenant during the Korean War, Burkett defended 45 courts martial. He holds a J.D. from the University of Oklahoma.

Printed in the United States
1065100003B/355-378

9 780939 965281